MANAGEMENT, WORK AND ORGANISATIONS

Series editors:
Gibson Burrell, The Management Centre, University of Leicester
Mick Marchington, Manchester Business School
Paul Thompson, Department of Human Resource Management, University of Strathclyde

The series of new textbooks covers the areas of human resource management, employee relations, organisational behaviour and related business and management fields. Each text has been specially commissioned to be written by leading experts in a clear and accessible way. The books contain serious and challenging material, take an analytical rather than prescriptive approach and are particularly suitable for use by students with no prior specialist knowledge.

The series is relevant for many business and management courses, including MBA and post-experience courses, specialist masters and postgraduate diplomas, professional courses and final-year undergraduate courses. These texts have become essential reading at business and management schools worldwide.

Published

Paul Blyton and Peter Turnbull **The Dynamics of Employee Relations** (3rd edn)
Sharon C. Bolton **Emotion Management in the Workplace**
Sharon Bolton and Maeve Houlihan **Searching for the Human in Human Resource Management**
Peter Boxall and John Purcell **Strategy and Human Resource Management**
J. Martin Corbett **Critical Cases in Organisational Behaviour**
Keith Grint **Leadership**
Irena Grugulis **Skills, Training and Human Resource Development**
Damian Hodgson and Svetlana Cicmil **Making Projects Critical**
Marek Korczynski **Human Resource Management in Service Work**
Karen Legge **Human Resource Management**: anniversary edition
Patricia Lewis and Ruth Simpson (eds) **Gendering Emotions in Organizations**
Helen Rainbird (ed.) **Training in the Workplace**
Jill Rubery and Damian Grimshaw **The Organisation of Employment**
Harry Scarbrough (ed.) **The Management of Expertise**
Hugh Scullion and Margaret Linehan **International Human Resource Management**
Adrian Wilkinson, Mick Marchington, Tom Redman and Ed Snape **Managing with Total Quality Management**
Colin C. Williams **Rethinking the Future of Work**
Diana Winstanley and Jean Woodall (eds) **Ethical Issues in Contemporary Human Resource Management**
Ruth Simpson and Patricia Lewis **Voice, visibility and the gendering of organizations**

For more information on titles in the Series please go to www.palgrave.com/busines/mwo

Invitation to authors

The Series Editors welcome proposals for new books within the Management, Work and Organisations series. These should be sent to Paul Thompson (p.thompson@strath.ac.uk) at the Dept of HRM, Strathclyde Business School, University of Strathclyde, 50 Richmond St Glasgow G1 1XT

Series Standing Order

If you would like to receive future titles in this series as they are published, you can make use of our standing order facility. To place a standing order please contact your bookseller or, in case of difficulty, write to us at the address below with your name and address and the name of the series. Please state with which title you wish to begin your standing order.

Customer Services Department, Macmillan Distribution Ltd
Houndmills, Basingstoke, Hampshire RG21 6XS, England

Voice, visibility and the gendering of organizations

Ruth Simpson

Brunel Business School, Brunel University

and

Patricia Lewis

Kent Business School, University of Kent

First published 2007 by
PALGRAVE MACMILLAN
Houndmills, Basingstoke, Hampshire RG21 6XS and
175 Fifth Avenue, New York, N.Y. 10010
Companies and representatives throughout the world

PALGRAVE MACMILLAN is the global academic imprint of the Palgrave Macmillan division of St. Martin's Press, LLC and of Palgrave Macmillan Ltd. Macmillan® is a registered trademark in the United States, United Kingdom and other countries. Palgrave is a registered trademark in the European Union and other countries.

ISBN-13: 978–1–403–99057–0
ISBN-10: 1–403–99057–3

This book is printed on paper suitable for recycling and made from fully managed and sustained forest sources. Logging, pulping and manufacturing processes are expected to conform to the environmental regulations of the country of origin.

A catalogue record for this book is available from the British Library.

A catalog record for this book is available from the Library of Congress.

10   9   8   7   6   5   4   3   2   1
16   15   14   13   12   11   10   09   08   07

Printed and bound in China

Contents

List of figures

1

Introducing voice and visibility in gender and organization studies

Introduction

This book is about gender and organizations. However, in a departure from other work in the area, we adopt an approach to the study of gender which draws on two interrelated concepts: voice and visibility. These concepts have been used in different ways in the gender/organization literature as well as in the wider social sciences. However, we argue that their potential as analytic principles has not been fully realized and we accordingly draw on these concepts to analyse developments in the field. In so doing we present a 'framework' based on 'surface' and 'deep' conceptualizations which forms the organizing principle of the book. In applying this distinction, and by exploring contradictions and areas of commonality, we critically assess the different theoretical perspectives and throw new light on the growing and increasingly diverse field of gender and organization studies (GOS).

In this respect, the book does two things. First it brings together the somewhat fragmented ways in which voice and visibility have been used in the gender and organization literature to present a comprehensive account of their explanatory potential. Secondly, we consolidate this potential within our framework, which we argue can be used not only as an organizing principle but as a basis for exploring specific phenomena and for highlighting gaps in interpretation within the field. In so doing, we both draw on and move outside the three feminist perspectives (liberal, radical and post-structuralist) dominant within GOS and through which the manifestation of gender in organizations has been conventionally read. While previous work has tended to treat these perspectives on gender as analytically and conceptually distinct, we suggest that through voice and visibility we can usefully explore overlaps and interconnections as well as contradictions between them.

Voice and visibility in gender and organization studies

The concepts of voice and visibility have been widely used in the social sciences. In both politics (Hirschman, 1970) and employment studies (Turnley & Feldman, 1999; Bowen & Blackmon, 2003; Edmonson, 2003) the concept of voice has been used, for example, to analyse how citizens articulate their critical opinions as well as how employees react to perceived injustices or wrong doing in the employment relationship. Drawing on some of the above work, voice and visibility have been used in gender and organization studies to analyse inequality and exclusion and to explore the absence of women from organizational research. Hearn (1994), Morgan (1992) and Gherardi (1995), for example, have challenged the 'gender neutral' stance of early work in organization studies, which failed to recognize that organizational practices and processes could be seen as gendered, and which consequently rendered gender differences invisible. The growth of GOS is therefore a welcome addition to the field of organizational behaviour in that it has given voice to women's experiences and has made visible the gendered nature of organizational practices.

Here, voice and visibility have been common themes. In terms of the former, what has become known as 'women's voice' literature has sought to redress the absence and neglect of women in organizational theorizing, to hear their accounts of work experiences and to incorporate their values. This has included a focus on the qualities that women bring to the organizational context as well as the challenges they face. Such work has explored how leadership styles of women differ from, and are often seen as more effective than, those of men (e.g. Rosener, 1990; Ferrario, 1991) as well as gender differences in career orientation (Nicholson & West, 1988; Burke & McKeen, 1994) and the barriers women face at work (Marshall, 1984; Coe, 1992; Ibarra, 1993; Burke et al., 1995; Oakley, 2000; Powell, 2000). Through this literature, women's voices have thus been included in organizational theory and research.

The concept of visibility has also been drawn on extensively. Kanter (1977), in one of the earliest work on women in organizations, explored the visibility of 'token' women working in male-dominated occupations and the implications of this visibility for their relationships at work and experiences as managers. As Kanter suggests, women are often disadvantaged by their token status – forced into a narrow set of stereotypical roles and largely excluded from the dominant group culture. Visibility emerged in her study as a 'burden' for women who often responded by trying to become invisible – avoiding conflict, for example, by not being too successful in work assignments.

More recently, work on gender in organizations has drawn on concepts of silence and invisibility (the antitheses of voice and visibility) to highlight the gendered nature of organizations and organizational processes. Here the focus is more on men and masculinity rather than women's experiences and values. Drawing on voice, recent work has highlighted how discourses of masculinity silence competing meanings. The concept of discourse captures how we see the world and make sense of reality. Discourse influences and shapes behaviour by helping to produce and constitute identities and interests. By setting limits and creating a system of 'exclusion, interdiction and prohibition' (Gordon, 2002), discourse defines the norms of acceptable behaviour and reasoning. Masculine discourses thus refer to ways of interpreting reality which draw on and reflect values and attitudes culturally associated with masculinity and which silence other competing discourses based on alternative values such as emotions, empathy and care.

At the same time, men and masculinity are often rendered 'invisible' because men are seen to stand for humanity in general and their experiences are consequently 'universalized'. Following from Foucault, work on the link between normativity and in(visibility) suggests that men in particular have maintained their position of power partly because they represent the normative standard case. We cannot question or interrogate what we take for granted and is hidden from view. As a result men, masculinity and their attendant privileges, hidden within the norm, are invisible and evade scrutiny. Therefore, while women have been 'hidden from history' (Mills, 2002) and, until recently, from theorizing around organizational practices and processes, men have also been invisible. However, the invisibility that men experience signifies not an absence or a 'weak presence' as in the case of women, but a 'strong presence' in that invisibility emanates from the transparency that accompanies the norm. This has rendered invisible the strong presence and salience of gender and gendered practices in organizations.

Surface and deep conceptualizations of voice and visibility

The above work suggests we need to 'unpick' the concepts of voice and visibility in order to incorporate and explore their respective 'opposites': silence and invisibility. On this basis, we make use of 'surface' and 'deep' conceptualizations – where surface refers to voice/visibility and to *states* of inequality while deep incorporates silence/invisibility and underlying *processes* which maintains that silence and keeps certain issues hidden from view. We therefore distinguish between surface states of voice which describes fairly static situations of inequality and neglect and the deep, more dynamic processes of silencing that occur around different discursive regimes. Equally, we argue for a differentiation between surface, more static states of exclusion and difference that run through much of the work on visibility associated with the problems of 'token' status and deep processes of maintaining power through the dynamic relationship between and struggles around invisibility and the norm.

These distinctions – between surface and deep conceptualizations of voice and visibility – allow us to both frame the literature and to explore some of the dynamics that manifest at their interface. Thus, we shall position liberal feminist inspired women's voice literature against post-structuralist accounts of discourse which seek to uncover the privileging of any voice. Similarly, we shall see how visibility and invisibility can be both a privilege and a burden – and how groups who have enjoyed the privileges of an invisible status are now seeking the benefits of being outside the norm. At the same time, we shall explore commonalities as well as differences between respective surface accounts (women's voice and work on token status) and those at a deep level (silencing and struggles around the norm). In this respect, we draw on their location within the feminist perspectives.

'Surface' voice, visibility and feminist theory

The conceptualization of voice and visibility briefly mapped out above are embedded within the three feminist perspectives conventionally drawn upon within GOS. In this context feminist theory is commonly organized around the frameworks of liberal feminism, radical feminism and post-structural feminism. Each has its roots in a different tradition or theoretical orientation.

Liberal feminism and surface accounts of voice and visibility

Liberal feminism has, as the name implies, its roots in the liberal political tradition based on principles of liberty and individualism. Here, the aim is to achieve a just society, allowing individuals to exercise free will and 'to fulfil themselves through a system of individual rights' (Calas & Smircich, 1996) as they engage, in a fair and equitable manner, in healthy competition for scarce resources (income, wealth, job opportunities). Equality can be achieved by freeing women from oppressive gender roles within existing and gender neutral institutional structures – through, for example, equal pay, equal opportunities, access to childcare and the elimination of gender stereotypes (Tong, 1998).

Rather than seeing a denial of difference between men and women as the only route to gender justice, as in early liberal feminism, later feminists argued that some account had to be taken of women's different circumstances – not least the fact that they bear children. Research therefore began to move away from seeing women as the same as men, to focus on difference and to make comparisons between men and women in terms of inequality and discrimination (Alvesson & Due Billing, 1997).

This focus on gender difference has informed much of women's voice research as well as work on the effects of visibility associated with numerical disadvantage. These surface conceptualizations focus on states of inequality: one demands that we listen to women and hear their accounts and experiences while the other explores material consequences of numerical imbalance. Both make explicit or implicit comparisons with men and focus, as with liberal feminism, on creating a level playing field for women through equal opportunity initiatives within what are seen as gender neutral organizational structures. According to this view, equality initiatives would allow women's voices to be heard and their experiences and needs to be incorporated into the organization. Equally, problems of visibility would dissipate with increased female participation so that women were no longer minorities in the organization. Surface accounts of voice and visibility, therefore, can be seen to have been informed by the liberal feminist tradition.

Radical feminism and surface accounts of voice and visibility

While liberal feminism ignores the maleness of the standard point of reference so that women are compared with the 'male' norm and often deemed deficient as a result, radical feminism is based on a rejection of the male standpoint and on the positive construction of feminist alternatives. Moreover, while liberal feminists attempt to reduce the impact of difference (e.g. by encouraging policies to allow women to compete on the same terms as men), radical feminists foreground and celebrate that difference and privilege female voices and experiences. The first and fundamental theme of radical feminism is that women as a group are oppressed by men as a group and that patriarchy is the oppressing structure of male domination (e.g. Firestone, 1970; Walby, 1997). Radical feminism therefore seeks to make visible male control as it is exercised in every sphere of women's lives.

Rather than calling for the *reformation* of existing institutions and structures, as under liberal feminism, radical feminism promotes their *transformation* on the grounds that they represent, irrespective of any equal opportunity polices and procedures, systems of male domination. Patriarchy, the domination of women by men, underpins all institutions and structures and societies are structured by the hierarchical differences between men and women. As Ferguson (1984) argues, women should mould their own structures according to feminine principles based, for example, on cooperation and friendships – the basis of a new order which does not subordinate women or their interests.

While we have identified women's voice literature as mainly liberal feminist in orientation, other aspects contain influences from radical feminism. This can be seen in some of the work on leadership (e.g. Rosener, 1990), a key strand of women's voice literature to be discussed in the next chapter, which contains radical feminist influences through a shared valorization and privileging of the feminine. Work on female-oriented leadership styles, for example, present, along the lines argued by Rosener (1990) and Ferguson (1984), women's skills and attributes (of facilitation, cooperation, team-working) as 'superior' to those of men (often based on hierarchical notions of 'command and control'). However, the strength of this influence may be modified by the fact that such research seeks to promote women's 'ways of doing' within *existing* (rather than transformed) organizational structures and so can be seen in this respect to be adhering more to reformist than radical principles.

Women's voice literature thus combines liberal feminism, with its focus on equality of opportunity, with some radical feminist principles through the privileging of the feminine in some leadership research. Work on visibility by contrast is more fundamentally liberal feminist in orientation. These accounts assume, along the lines of liberal feminism, neutral organizational structures in that an increase in numbers of women would, it is argued, eventually reduce female disadvantage. For radical feminists, these structures are fundamentally patriarchal – an increase in numbers would not in any way alter the patriarchal 'map' of the organization.

'Deep' voice, visibility and feminist theory: post-structuralist accounts

While women's voice literature, work on 'token' status and liberal feminist perspectives in general seek to show that women are different from men and have different experiences, they do not question the privileging and invisibility of the norm against which women are often measured or the influence of discursive practices which can eliminate issues from speech and sound. This is largely (but not exclusively) the province of post-structuralism and is concerned with our 'deep' conceptualization of voice and visibility.

Radical feminism goes some way to consider these deeper issues by looking beneath the surface at patriarchal power relations and challenging the supposed gender neutrality of organizational structures and processes. Ferguson (1984), for example, uses the concept of discourse to demonstrate how male thinking, attitudes and behaviours are written into organizations so that they seem acceptable and rendered invisible as 'normal' – an argument that has an alignment with our 'deep' understanding of voice and visibility in organizations. Post-structuralists also use discourse to uncover patriarchal power relations and to focus on deeper phenomenon than 'surface states' of exclusion, difference or neglect but go further by conceptualizing power as dispersed within discourse – powerful because they define our views of the world – and by exploring how discursive regimes are drawn upon in the formation of (gender) identity.

For post-structuralists, ideologies and discourses of gender take precedence over structural implications of numbers or equality of opportunity. As we have seen, the concept of discourse captures the significance of signs, labels, expressions and rhetoric that serve to shape our thinking, attitudes and behaviour and through which we construct meanings. Therefore, rather than supporting the possibility of a universal objective knowledge (such as stable understandings of masculinity and femininity supported by liberal and radical feminism), post-structuralists point to the unstable nature of knowledge and its openness to a plurality of often conflicting interpretations. Moreover, the power relations embedded in such claims mean that some interpretations can be privileged over others, reflecting and supporting the interests of dominant groups.

Further, in contrast to both liberal and radical feminism for which gender is a solid fact related to biology, gender identity for post-structuralists is contingent, fluid and fragmentary. In other words gender identity has no solid, material reality but needs to be reproduced on an ongoing basis. Gender is dynamic in that it is actively produced in day-to-day interactions in specific contexts. Gender identity and how it is experienced at a subjective level (how it feels to be a man, how it feels to be a woman) is made up of a variety of different discourses and so will vary in different contexts and different institutions. Therefore, rather than having unitary definitions of masculinity and femininity, post-structuralism recognizes that there are a number of different masculinities and femininities which are produced in different contexts, with some being more dominant or privileged than others. This perspective accordingly has a particular focus on masculinity as a privileged discourse, how it silences and cross-cuts other discourses and how it can be hidden, and hence evade scrutiny and interrogation, within the norm. These fundamental issues are captured in 'deep' understandings of visibility and voice.

The influence of radical feminism

Surface conceptualizations of voice and visibility are thus heavily influenced by liberal feminism while 'deep' conceptualizations have roots in post-structuralism. At both levels we have seen the influence of radical feminism. Radical feminism can be understood as a bridge between these two perspectives, influencing both and linking surface and deep.

From the discussion above, this influence can be seen in two ways. First, while early liberal feminism sought to gain equal status and *similarity* with men based on an unproblematic male norm, later work influenced by the radical feminist valorization of the feminine over the masculine, focused on ways in which women were *different from* men. One key impact of radical feminism therefore has been through the central place that has now been given to difference in considerations of gender that can be seen within both liberal and post-structuralist accounts.

Secondly, the influence of radical feminism can be seen in its recognition of the power of male discourse, developed by Ferguson (1984), to silence women's voices – an issue developed further by post-structuralists as they consider how discursive regimes define organizational arenas. Both see the difficulties encountered by women as part of a gendering of organizations that circumscribe or marginalize feminine discourse in favour of the masculine and where gender and gender issues are rendered invisible through the overwhelming presence of masculinity. However, as we have seen, post-structuralism has moved far from some of these initial roots. While radical feminism conceptualizes a single source of power in the form of patriarchy, for post-structuralists power is dispersed within discourse. It is not about the privileging of the male voice, as under radical feminism, but rather the dynamics that underpin the privileging of any voice – male or female. Therefore, while it is possible to identify the 'seed corn' of radical feminism within post-structuralist accounts, there is considerable divergence in understandings of gender and power.

Overall, while radical feminism is drawn on less extensively than either liberal feminism or post-structuralism, it has to a greater or lesser extent influenced both perspectives. This influence is highlighted in our reading of GOS through the 'lenses' of surface and deep conceptualizations of visibility and voice.

The structure of the book

In the following chapters we build up our framework of voice and visibility briefly outlined above. In the next chapter (Chapter 2) we present a surface conceptualization of voice, based on the need to redress the state of absence and neglect of women's voices and to bring in their voices and experiences. In Chapter 3 we go beneath surface accounts of voice to consider the power of discourse in suppressing and silencing competing meanings. Chapter 4 considers surface accounts of visibility as states of exclusion and difference and outlines the work on men and women as 'tokens' within their organizations. Chapter 5 concerns the privileges and invisibility that accompanies the norm, men's quest for visibility and its association with backlash discourses. In Chapter 6 we explore masculinity studies through 'surface' and 'deep' conceptualizations of voice and visibility and go some way to 'bring masculinity studies in' to a more generalized account of gender. Our concluding chapter (Chapter 7) draws together the different strands of theorizing into our framework and examines contradictions and paradox as a way of highlighting voice and visibility's explanatory potential.

We do not wish to overstate the framework in terms of its analytical powers. We see it more as an interpretive and heuristic device than a tool of analysis. In the following chapters we thus review and through the framework bring a measure of coherence to the diverse literatures in the field. Beyond this modest endeavour, however, we also hope to more fully exploit the potential of voice and visibility as explanatory concepts and, through their deployment, to re-invigorate some literatures in terms of their current significance, uncover specific relationships and point to interpretive gaps within some feminist research. Thus, we highlight in Chapter 2 the special contribution of women's voice literature (easily dismissed perhaps as somewhat lacking in critical rigour) on solution and resolution discourses as women make sense of the effects of difference in their life experiences; in Chapter 6 we uncover specific relationships through the concept of invisibility between masculinity, privilege and 'backlash' while in Chapter 7 we highlight possible interpretive gaps, through deep conceptualizations of voice and visibility, within work on gender and entrepreneurship. We accordingly hope to open up the potential of voice and visibility within the literature both in terms of providing a new lens through which to 'read' its diverse strands and in terms of pointing to new possibilities of inquiry.

2

Women's voices: a surface state of absence and neglect

Introduction

Are women the new men?

'Girls on top' discourses suggest that women are both psychologically and physically stronger than men. They are smarter, more socially adept and more successful at school and work; they are in touch with their feelings and with those of others – and they live longer. Amid this 'triumphalism' about women and female values, popular media coverage presents women as 'taking over the world' – moving steadily up the career ladder, earning more than their less fortunate male peers and managing both family and work. As the Daily Mail has commented: 'The world could soon be under the control of some remarkably superior beings' (*The Guardian*, 1999). Men by contrast are seen as the problem – known for anti-social activities (mugging, joy riding, crimes of violence), for their inadequate parenting or for out of date command and control type attitudes at work.

Where did this 'female supremacy' discourse come from? We argue in this chapter that it has emerged out of debates concerning the absence and neglect of women's voices, not only in terms of the lack of women in influential positions within the public sphere but also in terms of attaching value to women's difference. In the context of gender and work, what has come to be known as 'women's voice literature' has sought to give voice to women's experiences – to hear their accounts of their working lives and to understand their values. This work, as a 'surface' level conceptualization, views inequality as a *state of absence and neglect*. Early work on organization studies, for example, focused almost exclusively on men as the universal case to the neglect of women's voices and values. If considered at all, the experiences of women were viewed as deviant or problematic for organizations. This is illustrated in classic texts such as *Organization Man* (Whyte, 1956) and *Men who Manage* (Dalton, 1959) which, while ignoring gender, were gendered in their assumptions of the centrality of masculinity in organizational life. As Gilligan points out in relation to the 'phallocentric' model of human development:

> We have listened for centuries to the voices of men and the theories of development that their experiences informs, so we have come more recently to notice not only the silence of women but the difficulty of hearing what they say when they speak . . . The failure to see the different reality of women's lives and to hear the difference in their voices stems in part from the assumption that there is a single mode of social expression and interpretation. (1982: 173)

The aim of women's voice literature therefore has been to redress this 'lack' and to bring women's voices into the study and practice of organizations.

Such work has sought to show that women manage, speak, learn or negotiate in a different (but not inferior) way (Fondas, 1997) and that they encounter different problems from men. One important strand of such work has presented women's difference as an asset – of value to and increasingly valued by organizations and managers. As such it has contributed to popular representations of women as 'winners' in the modern workplace. Furthermore, as we argue in this chapter, women's voice literature has had a powerful influence on current conceptualizations of gender as a problem that has been 'solved' and has contributed towards the uptake of resolution discourses around merit and individual choice. This influence has largely been underestimated by academics and researchers in the area.

The female advantage

As we saw in the last chapter, liberal feminists recognize difference but have sought through equality initiatives to diminish its impact on women's lives. Much of the prolific work on women in management (e.g. Marshall, 1984; Coe, 1992; Ibarra, 1993; Burke et al., 1995; Oakley, 2000; Powell, 2000), a strand of women's voice research, has documented the ways in which women differ from men in terms of remuneration, career progress and career barriers. Gender is seen as a variable in charting differences between men and women within a framework of equality and where those differences are generally presented in a non-hierarchical way. Women in management literature has accordingly focused largely on the problems women face in managerial careers, with the explicit aim of removing gender-based barriers to career success.

A more radical approach has been to recognize and value rather than attempt to diminish difference. In other words, it has sought to foreground and celebrate that difference and to privilege female voices and experiences. From the perspective of the 'female advantage' or 'pro-women's voice', women have much to offer in terms of skills, attributes and leadership styles. Difference has been taken as women's strengths (Vinkenburg et al., 2000) highlighting the special contribution that women's uniquely female experience can offer as managers and leaders (Alimo-Metcalfe, 1994).

Transformational leadership

In this context, Rosener (1990) has argued that women tend to adopt a 'transformational' leadership style, encouraging subordinates to transform their self-interest into the interests of the group. Thus women lead through participation, power sharing and information exchange – reflective of their capacity for communication (Tannen, 2001; Belenky et al., 1997) and of their orientation towards responsibility and care (Gilligan, 1982). Similarly, in a study of managers, Ferrario and Davidson (1991) found that women had a more 'team based' approach than men – with others (e.g. Davidson & Cooper, 1983, 1984; Marshall, 1984; Fagenson, 1993) suggesting that women have a less hierarchical relationships-oriented style that displays more understanding and sympathy for others. Women therefore tend to view power as a capacity that stems from and is directed to the whole community' (Ferrario, 1994) rather than as an ability to control, an orientation shared by many men.

This more interactive approach encourages participation by enhancing people's self-worth and inclusion, where the leaders' power is ascribed to interpersonal skills and charisma. By contrast, men are seen to prefer a 'transactional' leadership style (Rosener, 1990), based on qualities of autonomy, independence and instrumentality, in which leadership is seen as a series of transactions with subordinates, exchanging rewards for services rendered and punishment for inadequate performance. Here, power is drawn not from interpersonal skills and charisma but from the formal status and authority in the organization.

Transformational leadership and the modern work context

The 'feminine' orientation to power is seen by the special contribution approach as an asset that is well suited to the modern work environment. Increased competition, a new customer focus and the growth of services have demanded a different style with a need for skills such as good communication, participation and team work traditionally associated with 'feminine' management (Due Billing & Alvesson, 1989). By calling upon skills and attributes associated with femininity, the practice of managing in the contemporary workplace has therefore been seen to be increasingly reflective of a feminine ethos. The classical, 'masculine' notion of managerial work as consisting of 'planning, ordering, directing and controlling' (Fondas, 1996: 288) with the associated need for 'hard' skills such as data analysis, business planning and financial control, may be giving way to a need for cooperation, the building of relationships and responsiveness to others (Kanter, 1989; Alvesson, 1998).

Competitive advantage in the marketplace may accordingly be increasingly dependent upon skills of cooperation and a shared influence, on the ability to build relationships with others and on the effectiveness of egalitarian partnerships both within and outside the organization. In that women are seen to have preferences for relationships and for ethics of care (Gilligan, 1982; Belenky et al., 1997) as well as for connectedness rather than separateness in their styles of communication (Tannen, 2001), they are presented as being well placed (unlike their more instrumentally minded, command- and control-oriented male colleagues) to succeed in the modern work environment. In other words, they are positioned in this context to become winners as 'new men'.

Female advantage and the (man)agement project

While we might applaud this supposed new era for women, there have been many voices of scepticism and concern. As Ariel Levy (author of *Female Chauvinist Pigs*) has queried: 'When did we win? We don't have equal pay for equal work; we don't have equal representation in government . . . so when exactly did we win?' (*The Guardian*, 21 June 2006). This questions the exact nature of the advantages of 'female advantage' for women. In the context of organizations, several reservations about the pro-women's voice literature have been raised.

First, at an empirical level, it is by no means clear that women do have a style that is radically different from that which is adopted by men. Several studies have found no significant gender differences (e.g. Eagly & Johnson, 1990; Butterfield & Grinnel, 1999) while others suggest difference *between* women may be just as important. Kanter (1977) for example found that while women in more junior roles may adopt a transformational style, senior women distanced themselves from any valued feminine traits that they may have earlier endorsed and adopted a more masculine approach.

More fundamentally as Due Billing and Alvesson ·(2000) argue, this per-spective, while challenging traditional 'masculine' notions of hierarchy, man-agement and leadership, runs the danger of essentializing gender, reinforcing stereotypical views of women (e.g. as caring, nurturing, cooperative) and encouraging negative attitudes towards women when they step out of these stereotypical roles. Eagly et al. (1992), for example, found that women were valued more negatively than men when adopting an authoritarian style and that they were seen as bossy and overbearing. Promoting the female advantage may consequently reduce the leadership repertoire of women, tying them down to a narrow set of leadership ideals and behaviours (Due Billing & Alvesson, 2000). Moreover, as Ashcraft and Mumby (2004) argue, these orientations, interaction patterns and associated perceptions rather than facilitating women's progress in organizations, can act as a barrier if women enact behaviours or draw on language that signify that they are not fitted for what is often seen as the 'cut and thrust' of senior management roles.

The nurturing image associated with this leadership style may also result in women being involved in people-oriented areas of business (human resources, customer service) which are often dead-end career tracks (Ferrario, 1991). These skills rarely form the basis for promotion decisions but remain invisible and unrewarded. In support of this, there is little evidence to suggest that the so-called 'feminization' of management has led to more women in senior positions. Women are still in the minority at all management levels and the further up the hierarchy the greater the disparity. For example, only 3.4 per cent of board members in the United Kingdom are women (Singh & Vinnicombe, 2005). Moreover, as Calas and Smircich (1992) argue, trends towards 'valuing the feminine' simply restate existing management practices under a different name: they give the impression of valuing women and an illusion of equal opportunity while obstructing an examination of the gendered nature of management. In essence management remains fundamentally 'male'.

A development of the above argument concerns a possible 're-masculinization' of management through the discourse of and practices associated with female advantage – a theme we revisit in the next chapter. This has been demonstrated in the screening out of the feminine in the language and prescriptions of modern management texts (Fondas, 1997) as well as in the use to which the associated ('feminine') skills and attributes have been put (Fletcher, 1994). As Fletcher argues, attributes of self reflection, empathy and empowerment have been captured and put to instrumental use by organizations through, for example, processes and practices associated with team working, with more contextually sensitive decision making and with a holistic and integrative approach to problem solving. In other words, female advantage has been brought into the organization and used to add value in the 'masculine' managerial project of efficiency, performance and output. In so doing, the female voice has been de-gendered and its transformative power 'castrated'. As Fletcher states:

> using these relational qualities instrumentally will benefit all involved – organizations will be more effective, female diversity will be recognised for its 'value added', and males will be encouraged to adopt these feminine characteristics. These positive outcomes are not problematic. What...is problematic is that incorporating women's voice into the management literature in this way – that is revisioning relational skills as instrumentally useful in addressing current organizational problems – actually silences that very element of women's voice that could serve to challenge masculine ways of organizing. More specifically, it suggests that using feminine relational skills in a masculine instrumental way castrates these qualities, qualitatively changing their nature and neutralizing their power to challenge the status quo. (78–79)

In short, women's relational strengths within the 'female advantage' are re-presented as instrumentally useful – captured and re-masculinized in the drive for performance, competitiveness and control. In so doing its powerful essence is rendered invisible and the female voice, with its potential to challenge patriarchal structures and to effect radical change, is silenced.

Women's voices and constructions of difference

As we have seen, women's voice literature is constructed around concepts and meanings of difference. Women in management research, as one strand of this work, is largely organized around the liberal feminist principle of 'neutral difference', that is, a non-hierarchical conceptualization where difference is highlighted (charted, measured) in order to reduce its impact on women's organizational lives. Through equal opportunities designed to overcome career barriers, differences diminish such that men and women compete on the same basis. By contrast pro-women's voice leadership research, with its radical feminist influences, conceives of a hierarchical difference with the feminine valorized over the masculine. Rather than seeking to diminish its impact, difference is accordingly celebrated and valued. Both focus on *differences between* men and women and suggest a binary view of gender (male/female, masculine/feminine) supportive of stereotypical ideas of how men and women communicate and behave. However, as Ashcraft and Mumby (2004) point out, this represents a 'tired and problematic' view of difference in that it fails to challenge the assumptions that underpin these views.

As Ashcraft and Mumby (2004) argue, the binary divide supports an understanding of gender as a stable identity organized around biological sex or cultural membership which then assumes core group similarities. We all have presuppositions about the meaning, traits and attributes of category 'man' and 'woman'. These understandings and presuppositions then become the lens through which we subsequently 'read' gender behaviour. In other words, the behaviour of men and women is understood through a more general discourse of gender (Coates, 1998) and that discourse is subsequently invoked to explain the patterns and differences perceived. On this basis, it is not surprising that what we see (e.g. women's orientation towards relationships and care; men's orientation towards independence and instrumentality) often conforms to (stereo)type.

As we discuss further in the next chapter, rather than a trait or attribute attaching to the individual, recent work has explored how we 'do' gender and 'do' gender difference (West & Zimmerman, 2002) in our everyday lives. In this vein, as Butler (1999) argues, gender is performative in that feminine and masculine are not what we are or traits we have but effects we produce by way of what we do. Gender is therefore not an attribute of the individual as assumed by the women's voice perspective, but 'a set of repeated acts within a regulatory frame which congeal over time to produce the appearance or substance of a 'natural' kind of being' (Butler, 1999: 33). Becoming a man or a woman is not something that is accomplished once and for all but has to be constantly reaffirmed and publicly displayed by repeatedly performing particular acts in accordance with cultural norms which define masculinity and femininity.

This performative model sheds interesting light on gender differences in leadership style. These too are performance – the result of repeated acts (relating, communicating, managing, negotiating) by social actors who are striving to constitute themselves as 'proper' men and women in these roles. In so doing, they draw on cultural and other resources such as dress, body language, emotional expression as well as modes of communication.

In terms of the latter, research indicates distinct gender differences in communication styles. Women are more deferential than men. They listen more, are less likely to interrupt and tend to give affirmation to the speaker through gestures and body movement such as smiling and nodding (Tannen, 2001; Coates, 1998) – attributes that underpin their more transformational leadership style. Men by contrast are more likely to dominate conversations, to interrupt and to give directions – in other words to see leadership as a series of transactions with subordinates. However, as Coates argues, rather than assuming that people communicate the way they do because of who they already are (i.e. male/female), men and women become gendered and are who they are through, amongst other things, the way they talk, listen and make connections with others. In short, as West and Zimmerman (2002) point out, gender is 'constituted through interaction'.

This shifts the focus away from a simple cataloguing of differences between men and women to a more complex inquiry into how people use cultural, symbolic, linguistic and other resources to produce gender differentiation. Rather than being essentially caring, empathetic and relational in their leadership styles, women may draw on those attributes in day-to-day interactions as part of 'doing gender' in their leadership role. Rather than seeing difference as a 'static gap' between men and women, a more enlightened approach (Ashcraft & Mumby, 2004) might accordingly be to consider how discourse constructs difference, that is, how our taken for granted assumptions and presuppositions makes differentiation visible and how men and women draw on difference to construct their gendered selves.

The influence of women's voice literature

In attempting to redress the state of absence and neglect in terms of women's accounts and experiences of organizations, we have identified women's voice literature as a 'surface' conceptualization. As such, it can be charged with failing to go beneath these 'states' to explore underlying practices or processes – and the arguments presented above on the how difference is constructed are testimony to this 'lack'. On this basis it would be easy to dismiss the foundations, outcomes and prescriptions of women's voice research as overly simplistic and lacking in depth. However, this would be to miss the enormous impact that such work has had on the way men and women interpret difference in their everyday lives, how they make sense of the opportunities available to them and how they view the significance of choice.

Women's voice: a powerful metaphor

Certainly, on one level, the relevance of women's voice literature partly reflects the potency of its metaphorical base. Voice is a powerful figure of speech for many aspects of women's experiences. Voice suggests dialogue and interaction, being listened to and being heard while absence of voice captures lack of power and marginalization. Women often refer to losing or gaining voice as they reflect on aspects of their development as individuals (Belenky et al., 1997) inside and outside work. Simpson et al.'s (2005) study of MBA graduates, for example, found that confidence from the MBA experience was seen by many women to give them a 'voice' (as one woman commented – 'it helped me speak'). Women developed the self-assurance to verbalize – to make their views known, to put their ideas on the table in meetings and to discuss issues with senior staff.

In literature on gender and organizations, women are often seen to lack voice, their issues and grievances transformed into silence by more powerful (male) voices that marginalize and exclude them. Harlow et al. (1995) refer to these dominant voices as 'din'. Din is negative or oppressive noise (though as Harlow points out some silence can also be oppressive and therefore count as din) which crowds out those outside the dominant group, creating a 'silent agenda' of suppressed issues. The silent agenda is not heard because key voices have been drowned by the din of more powerful groups.

Silence and din

Silence and din refer to overt and covert gendered domination within organizations (Harlow et al., 1995). Din (which relates mainly but not exclusively to the overbearing nature of male voices) arises in the board-room and meetings, for example, where men's voices take over through force of numbers and through the often intimidating use of gendered language. Dominance in conversations through interruptions, put downs or topic change, seen as typically male communication styles (Cameron, 1995), is therefore din which serves to marginalize and exclude those (particularly women) to whom they speak.

On this basis, silence or lack of voice can be related to the passivity of the oppressed. Women often lose voice when confronted with the din of male voices in organizations. However, silence and din are not exclusively opposite. Silence, the absence of noise, can also be full of significant meaning. Silence can be the response of men or management to the din of demands for recognition and change – for example, the silence that often accompanies claims from women of sexual harassment (Collinson & Collinson, 1996). As Cameron (1995) has pointed out, men often ignore women when they talk and so control conversations. Silence can be a tool for the maintenance of domination and as such comprise din. At the same time, grievances of oppressed groups, while silenced by more powerful groups, can also be din. In this way, silence can therefore also be dominating while din can be the noise of the oppressed.

Voice therefore captures the literal (the ability to speak and command attention) and the abstract (inclusion, exclusion and power). As well as the influence that its agenda of *giving voice* to women in organizations has had on the significance now given to gender at work, the conceptual and metaphorical base of women's voice literature has also powerfully reflected women's experiences of 'silence and din' and has relevance for their claims to be listened to and understood.

Difference, sameness and the significance of choice

More fundamentally, women's voice literature and its underlying assumptions has had a powerful influence on the uptake of solution and resolution discourses among women as they manage the dichotomies and tensions within their everyday lives. These tensions relate partly to the simultaneous existence of sameness (based on equality of opportunity and merit) and difference (based on women's special contribution) discourses. As we have seen, equal opportunities and merit suggest that difference can be diminished and that women can compete on the *same basis* as men. With these policies intact men and women can effectively be treated as the same. However, 'girls on top' or special contribution discourses are based on the notion that women are *different* from men. In other words they are both different and the same – a contradiction that has implications for how women make sense of their lives.

A further source of tension concerns the conflict between these two discourses (merit/special contribution) and the disadvantage experienced by many women in the materiality of their organizational lives. In this respect, despite equality, merit and 'sameness' and despite special contribution and 'difference', women continue to earn less than men, are rarely seen in senior management teams and are often ghettoized into 'caring', service and/or non-strategic roles.

How do women manage these tensions? We argue in this section that these tensions are negotiated both *within* and *between* the two discourses of sameness and difference. First, women draw heavily on *one or other* as they recount their experiences and make sense of their lives. This they do in often conflicting and contradictory ways and despite evidence, in each case, to the contrary. Secondly, women move *between* and incorporate both discourses through the concept of choice. Both 'strategies' have been heavily influenced by women's voice perspective.

Themes of difference have been found to run through many women's accounts of their lives as they present themselves as having a special contribution to make. Ross-Smith et al. (2007) found that women managers saw themselves in gender stereotypical ways – as 'emotion specialists' offering support to others and, as such, as different from men. Similarly, Cliff et al. (2005) found that women drew on gender-stereotypic rhetoric to describe their approaches to business, even though (from the same study) no subsequent differences emerged. Women accordingly described their orientation in feminized relational 'people' oriented terms (one woman likened her business to a 'nurturing nest') and talked as if they organized and managed their firms in different ways from men. This is despite there being no evidence among the men and women in the study of gender difference in style.

By contrast, sameness discourse is evident in women's adherence to and belief in merit as the rationale behind their own and others' career success. Women thus frequently deny the salience of gender (and of difference/disadvantage) in their organizational lives (Piderit and Ashford, 2003), preferring a rhetoric of equal chance, hard work and reward for effort – despite evidence that difference and disadvantage do exist. Lewis (2006), for example, found that female entrepreneurs draw on an ideology of gender blindness and emphasize their similarity to the wider population of men demonstrating, in their perceptions of factors leading to success, a strong belief in the neutrality and meritocracy of the business world. The privileging of the male in business and the supremacy of masculine discourse within entrepreneurship are thus overlooked. Perhaps influenced by 'girls on top' discourses suggesting that prospects have never been so good, women accordingly deny disadvantage. As Lewis argues, this denial might assist women in gaining access to mainstream executive culture and avoid a damaging identification with gender and with difference from the norm.

Women thus draw on difference or on sameness, in often contradictory ways, as they make sense of their experiences. Women also move between sameness and difference through an emphasis on choice. Rhetoric around choice has considerable purchase in women's accounts of their lives. Women's ability to choose and the results of the choices they make are used to justify unequal outcomes and experiences. The significance of choice is supported by Hakim's (2000, 2002) preference theory which suggests that continued differences between men and women in the labour market are due to choices women make – for home-centred, work-centred or adaptive life styles (in the latter women choose to combine work with family through, for example, part-time work).

By drawing on the rhetoric around choice, women combine elements of sameness (choice implies equality of opportunity) and difference (the need for choice is based on difference; the results of choice lead to difference in outcomes). As Hakim argues, choice has become possible (and now central) in women's life plans because of successful equal opportunities policies, giving women equal access to most positions in the public arena. Choice is thus partly premised on the 'sameness' principle (without equal opportunities and some adherence to meritocracy women would effectively have no choice). Not all women, however, are work-centred and prioritize other aspects of their lives. Therefore, labour market and other outcomes are different from those of men. As Hakim states:

> Preference theory predicts that men will retain their dominance in the labor market, politics, and other competitive activities because only a minority of women are prepared to prioritise their jobs (or other activities in the public sphere) in the same way as men. (2002: 437)

Uptake and internalization of the rhetoric of choice help women negotiate the tensions between sameness and difference outlined above. Thus, if women are presented as having choice and if unequal outcomes can be presented as the result of choices they have made, then the impact (in the eyes of women) of discrimination or gender disadvantage can be diminished. Thus a voluntaristic element to difference is introduced: women have *chosen* an unequal outcome such as to enter a less strategic support management function, to work part-time or to take extended maternity leave. This helps to align 'girls on top' rhetoric with the reality of their lives and keeps intact the concept of equality and meritocracy to which many women, despite evidence to the contrary, strongly adhere.

Overall, the powerful influence of women's voice literature and its associated rhetoric can be seen in the prevalence and dominance of solution and resolution discourses. Women's voice accordingly provides both an answer to and an explanation of women's position in organizations. In terms of the former, rhetoric around equal opportunities and pro-women's voice discourses suggest that the barriers to success have been removed – and that the answer to the 'problem' of gender has been found (it has been 'solved'). Similarly, in terms of the latter, equal opportunities and an associated belief in merit help explain, through the concept of choice, any continuing difference and disadvantage (the problem of difference and disadvantage has been resolved).

Conclusion

We have presented women's voice literature and research as a 'surface' conceptualization, oriented towards redressing the absence and neglect of women's voices in organizations. In so doing, women's voice acknowledges the 'weak presence' of women and is based on the premise that a masculine bias lies at the heart of organizations and associated academic disciplines. By giving voice to difference, such work expresses the values of the female world and helps to include women. From this perspective, as Jansen and Davis (1998) point out, the goal of feminist research is to correct the 'distortions' associated with the female experience. Such work accordingly sees 'lack of voice' as a *state of absence and neglect*.

The women's voice perspective is grounded in the recognition of gender as a fairly fixed feature of identity, of gender difference as a 'static gap' based on comparisons with men (*difference between*) and of largely neutral organizational structures. However, this overlooks the dynamic nature of difference; how meanings attached to difference help construct gender identity as well as the gendered nature of bureaucratic structures and processes. In terms of the latter, solution and resolution discourses are premised on notions of a neutral bureaucracy where equal opportunities and merit are sufficient to overcome gender disadvantage and where individual choices are free and unconstrained. Equal opportunities, however, are unlikely to 'solve' gender disadvantage if the foundations of the organization as well as its processes and procedures are fundamentally flawed. Moreover, as McRae (2003) has argued, the choices women make are rarely 'free' but are constrained by cultural norms and circumstance. Perhaps more fundamentally, while women's voice literature helps us to hear women's accounts and to understand their values and experiences, it does not address the *process of silencing* that occurs. These processes, discussed in the next chapter, operate at a deeper, more fundamental level and help explain why some voices continue to go unheard.

We started this chapter with some popular representations of 'girls on top' and of women as 'new men'. We linked these conceptualizations to the influence of pro-women's voice literature which have promoted skills and attributes culturally associated with femininity as of value in contemporary organizations. This has been aptly demonstrated through transformational leadership research. Despite its limitations, we have argued that women's voice literature has been enormously influential in terms of the generalized uptake of solution and resolution discourses around difference and how the material consequences of difference are viewed. Its influence can be seen in the primacy afforded to merit and choice as 'mediators' in tensions experienced between the rhetoric and the reality of many women's lives.

3
Deep conceptualizations of voice: silencing within and through discourse

Introduction

This chapter explores 'deep' conceptualizations of voice. In other words, it considers how some voices are privileged over others and the significance of 'silence and din' (Harlow et al., 1995) in the production and maintenance of gender relations. We therefore distinguish between the 'surface' accounts of voice as discussed in Chapter 2 and, at this deeper level, power processes that mean some voices are heard over others. As such, we draw in greater depth on the concept of discourse, that is, signs, labels, expressions and rhetoric that serves to shape our thinking, attitudes and behaviour and, by creating meanings, help to frame concepts of 'normality'. Dominant ways of thinking and seeing, underpinned by an appropriate language, enable voices which support these meanings, to be heard while other, dissenting voices are silenced – as excessive, ridiculous or unreasonable. These processes are captured in our deep conceptualization of voice.

This approach is associated with post-structuralist interpretations, which move on from seeing gender as a category adhering to the individual or as a set of characteristics that are inherent or acquired through socialization. As we have seen, this 'static' view of gender underpins surface conceptualizations of voice and visibility, as well as liberal and radical feminist interpretations. Post-structuralist accounts, by contrast, see gender as dynamic, that is, actively produced through, for example, day–to-day interactions, and as contingent in that gender ultimately depends on context. This approach highlights the issues of complexity, ambiguity and fluidity in gender construction and recognizes the roles of agency as well as of institutions and social practices. Post-structuralists are interested to explore how gender is experienced at a subjective level as well as how gender dynamics emerge in different situations.

Rather than having unitary definitions of masculinity and femininity, as in earlier accounts associated with liberal and radical feminism, post-structuralism recognizes that there are a number of different masculinities and femininities which are produced in different contexts, with some being more dominant or privileged than others. There are, for example, dominant conceptualizations of 'what it means to be a man' (e.g. decisive, rational, in control) as well as dominant views of 'preferred' femininity (Connell, 2000) (passive, compliant, caring). These 'discourses' have a powerful impact on how we think and behave as well as on how we construct and reconstruct ourselves as gendered subjects.

The significance of discourse

Surface accounts of discourse

In Chapter 2, we made a brief reference to gender differences in communication styles. This drew implicitly on a concept of discourse as communication, which was seen to be ordered in fairly predictable ways. In this respect, Gilligan (1982), Belenky et al. (1997) and Tannen (2001) discuss the different communication styles of men and women and suggest that women approach communication as a means of building relationships. This in turn can support or reinforce certain 'transformational' leadership styles (Rosener, 1990) based on participation, power sharing and communication.

This 'modernist' approach sees gender as a stable category that transcends historical, cultural or institutional contexts – with discourse, in the form of communication style, acting as one of many possible variables of analysis within the organization. Organizations are thus seen as 'containers of discourse' (Grant et al., 2004). At this 'surface' level, therefore, the concept of 'discourse' describes, in a largely uncritical way, stable predictable communication styles as illustrated through gender difference. However, this conceptualization fails to problematize or interrogate the source of that difference (Ashcraft & Mumby, 2004) or to consider the role of discourse in the reproduction of power relations – issues taken up by post-structuralist orientations and which form the basis of our 'deeper' analysis.

Deep accounts of discourse

At a deeper level, post-structuralists draw on a broader and richer concept of discourse that goes beyond styles of communication. This concept incorporates varieties of 'texts' such as signs, labels, expressions and rhetoric that serve to shape our thinking, attitudes and behaviour and are implicated in how meaning is constructed and maintained. The focus of analysis, the text, signifies 'collections of interaction' (Grant et al., 2004), either oral, written or symbolic, which help to create social reality. It is through vocabulary, metaphor or narratives as well as through symbols (such as body language, office trappings or dress) that we construct meanings.

Therefore, rather than supporting the possibility of a universal objective knowledge (as in stable and 'essential' understandings of gender supported by liberal and radical feminism), post-structuralists interrogate such knowledge claims and highlight the power relations inherent in the constitution of those claims. Language, both written and spoken, far from conveying a stable reality, is open to multiple interpretations and, through inclusion and exclusion, can privilege some meanings and interpretations over others. In other words, discursive practices 'do not just describe things, they do things' (Potter & Wetherall, 1987: 6 cited in Grant et al., 2004), in particular they can reflect and support the interests of dominant groups and create or deny spaces for alternative orientations or meanings.

This deeper conceptualization of discourse goes beyond 'surface' accounts of gender differences in communication styles to explore the reproduction of power relations. For some 'discourse analysts', talk and written text 'stand alone' in that they are seen to form the basis of social interaction: an analysis of these forms of communication (discourse) can, on its own, lead to an understanding of social relationships often largely irrespective of the nature of the social institutions in which such communication takes place. As Alvesson and Karreman (2000) point out, such discourse stands in a relatively loose relationship with other, external, phenomena.

A more critical approach goes beyond the actual text and sees discourse as reflecting and creating social reality and associated 'power-knowledge relations' – whereby some forms of seeing the world take precedence and are valorized over others. In the last chapter we charted the powerful influence of discourses of equality, merit and choice on how women make sense of their lives and of their experiences. Discourse thus works as a 'structuring, constituting force' tightly framing subjectivity, practice or meaning (ibid). This approach, referred to as Critical Discourse Analysis (e.g. Mumby & Clair, 1997; Oswick et al., 2000) focuses on how discourse is used to maintain power relations and on the way discourses, past and present, can be a site of struggle over hegemonic meanings. Discourses around equal opportunities (through rhetoric of fairness, meritocracy, equality), for example, can conflict and vie with discourses around traditional masculinity (through rhetoric of bread-winners, toughness, commitment) and the appropriate 'placing' of men and women inside and outside the organization. Consequently, meanings about organizations can be framed by rhetorical strategies which in turn help structure and define organizational and management attitudes and practices (Fondas, 1997; Maddock, 1999; Leonard, 2002). 'Discursive regimes' therefore ascribe meaning to taken for granted concepts such as organization, management and gender (Fondas, 1997) and these meanings can maintain a 'tight control' (Kerfoot & Knights, 1998) over organizational life, while at the same time being the source and focus of resistance and struggle from alternative interests and orientations.

Gender as 'discursively produced'

Surface conceptualizations of voice and visibility seek to understand the factors that make up difference, where those characteristics are seen to be located in the individual – acquired inherently or through processes of socialization. Described by Ashcraft and Mumby (2004) as a 'tired' view of difference, this approach prevents us from seeing how gender structures 'distinctive domains of social experience' (West & Fenstermaker, 1995). In other words, surface explanations treat sex differences as an *explanation* rather than as an *analytical point of departure* (ibid). Furthermore, as we saw in Chapter 2, this approach views and makes sense of the behaviours that are seen to make up difference through wider gendered discourses, that is, through a lens that is already distorted by gendered assumptions. These assumptions and discourses are then invoked, circuitously, to explain that behaviour. A more fruitful focus of inquiry might be to consider how discourse constructs difference (Ashcraft & Mumby, 2004) or how language and voices are drawn upon and contribute to the performance and display of gender (Butler, 1990). In other words, such an inquiry would focus on how gender is 'discursively' produced.

From this more dynamic perspective, gender has been seen by some as an 'accomplishment' (e.g. West & Zimmerman, 2002), acted out or performed in day-to-day interactions according to prevailing norms and expectations. Through these interactions and through their repetition (Butler, 1999), such norms and expectations take on the semblance of universality and are seen to constitute what counts as 'knowledge' about gender, that is, they are considered to be 'normal' or 'natural' ways of doing gender and so help to legitimize and maintain the gender hierarchy. Butler refers to this process as 'performativity' whereby gender is seen as 'a set of repeated acts within a regulatory frame which congeal over time to produce the appearance or substance of a 'natural' kind of being' (1993: 33). Therefore, becoming a man or a woman has to be constantly reaffirmed and publicly displayed through repeated performances of gender, where these performances conform to (or sometimes actively resist) dominant definitions of masculinity and femininity. In this way, discourses and 'forms of signification' (Calas & Smircich, 1991) allow certain activities the claim of knowledge while others are not allowed. Such knowledge then helps make up what is widely accepted as 'masculinity' and femininity' and what are seen as normal behaviours of men and women.

Discourse and identity

Discourses help to define and shape social reality, to give it meaning. In that we are part of that reality, and given that we act out gender according to prevailing norms and expectations (i.e. discourses) it stands to reason that discourses also have the power to shape our sense of self. How we see ourselves as men and women therefore are products of discourse. As Clegg (1989) argues, through discursive practices such as talk, text, cognition, argumentation, representation, we construct our sense of self. We have recourse to a variety of 'texts' in the form of language, narratives, symbols to create our identities in different (local) situations which conform to (or resist) expectations. Highlighting the dynamic nature of gender construction, Martin (2003) distinguishes between gender practices (the class of discursive, cultural, narrative, bodily activities) that are available for people to draw on in an interaction and that conform to broader gender expectations and the practicing of gender (the doing, displaying, manoeuvring, narrating).

Men and women therefore construct each other through the two-sided dynamic of (discursively related) gendering practices and the practicing of gender. In this construction, as Martin points out, women's sense of self and confidence are impaired. This impairment, based on passivity and dependence where self denial and care of others is encouraged and valued, partly sustains the 'privileged and elevated' organizational masculinity (Kerfoot & Knights, 1998) which is aggressively competitive, goal driven and instrumental in the pursuit of success. This idealized conception of passive femininity silences women's authority in the organization and in so doing offers 'authority space' to men. As Kerfoot and Knights argue, many women struggle to achieve the feminine ideal, 'merging into the background thus enabling men to take control' while men struggle to attain the ideal of power, control and of rational, competitive success. Through competing discourses of masculinity and femininity and associated language, symbols and meanings, as well as daily interactions and performances, subjectivity and identity is negotiated and maintained. Identity is thus a project to be worked on – never total or complete as individuals labour in different contexts to fulfil norms and expectations of what it means to be woman or a man.

Dominant discourses: managerialism and masculinity

As we have seen, discourses stand in a dialectic and hierarchical relation to each other. Some meanings and interpretations are accordingly valorized and given priority over others. But this status of hegemony is not fixed – it has to be negotiated and reaffirmed on a day-to-day basis and will therefore be the focus of tension and conflict as other competing meanings challenge that dominant position. In this section, we consider two interrelated and intersecting discourses – those of managerialism (as a specific approach to management and administration) and of masculinity. Both discourses are powerful influences on our attitudes and practices inside and outside the work context. Both reject the 'feminine', drawing on meanings pertaining to rationality (Ross-Smith & Kornberger, 2004; Morgan, 1996) and sharing a preoccupation with accountability, direction and control (Kerfoot & Knights, 1993, 1998; Collinson & Hearn, 1994; Hearn, 1994; Connell, 1995, 2000; Kerfoot & Whitehead, 1998).

Managerialism comprises a set of beliefs and practices that are based on the assumption that management can offer solutions to organizational problems and that these solutions will improve organizational effectiveness and performance. As Collinson and Hearn (1994) point out, these beliefs and practices are prioritized over others so as to become the norm. The managerial prerogative over key decisions can be seen in the spread of managerial discourse and practice into areas previously governed by ideologies relating to service and care, such as education, health or volunteering.

In universities in the United Kingdom, for example, managerialist ideas are evident in practices that have arisen as a result of the government sponsored research assessment exercise (RAE) where universities are ranked according to the quality of their research. The setting of objectives in terms of research outputs (e.g. journal articles, book chapters, books) targets for research grants and the ranking of publications together with the calculation of a numerically based research profile for staff are common practices in the run-up to the six-yearly exercise. This drive towards an individualistic and market-based rationality, incorporating an unproblematic belief in accountability, efficiency and control (Grey et al., 1996) with its associated rhetoric of quality and value for money, has shifted earlier discourses around collegiality, academic freedom and scholarship (as well as dusty images of academics pursuing quirky, esoteric research).

In so far as these (managerial) meanings can find purchase within dominant conceptions of masculinity, there is a close association between the two. Accordingly, managerialist initiatives such as performance reviews and performance targets have been linked to a 'compulsive masculinity' (Kerfoot & Knights, 1993) through the quest for power and control (Kerfoot & Knights, 1993, 1998; Hearn, 1994). Gendered activities and gendered values are involved in the drive to achieve corporate objectives through managerialist processes such as codification, judgement, measurement and discipline (as illustrated in the example of the RAE above) – all of which conform with activities and attributes which are seen to be dominantly male (Connell, 2000). Discursive practices and assumptions that underpin the rationale and performance of managerialism are therefore heavily gendered and converge with masculinity in the preoccupation with power, accountability and control.

Managerialism also has close associations with the norms of rationality. Instrumental rationality, based on the most efficient means to achieve given (often monetary based) ends, forms the cornerstone of managerial initiatives outlined above. As Morgan (1996) points out, instrumental rationality has close connections with qualities considered masculine – in particular efficiency, effectiveness and calculating self interest. As Bologh, cited in Ross-Smith and Kornberger (2004), argues, this process:

> implies reliance on precise measurements, comparison and quantitative calculation of costs and benefits . . . Instrumental calculating rationality brings with it qualities considered masculine: smart and decisive self-determination or free, confident aggressive action. (1990: 126)

Managerialism and rationality therefore are powerful discourses that underpin and permeate most (public sector, private sector, not-for-profit sector) organizations and are closely aligned with dominant notions of masculinity. The two discourses (masculinity, managerialism) coincide and, however problematic, are mutually supportive – and it is partly through such support that they maintain their hegemonic status. By contrast, discourses of managerialism and femininity diverge (Kerfoot & Knights, 1998). Contradictions and tensions therefore exist between discourses of managerialism (based on rationality, power and control) and of femininity (based on emotionality, passivity and dependence). Recently, however, discourses of femininity have challenged the hegemonic status of these 'masculine' ideas.

Challenging the hegemonic discourse: the feminization of management

We have established so far that social reality is shaped by power-knowledge relations established in discourse (Alvesson & Karreman, 2000). In other words, what we take as 'fact' or as 'normal' is heavily influenced by assumptions and values, by the language that is used and by the manner in which such meanings are conveyed. We have also intimated that to maintain its 'hold' on our thinking and behaviour, dominant discourses must be able to suppress and silence other, contradictory or competing meanings. In this way, as in our example of UK universities above, a market-based rhetoric around quality, efficiency and value for money can legitimize through their appeals to the reasonable, the sensible and the sound, a variety of (controlling, accounting) measures and so suppress alternative orientations – based, for example, on personal fulfilment or care. Privileged ways of talking and being, through linguistic processes such as rhetoric and naming, can consequently form the site of struggle over hegemonic interpretations (Fondas, 1997; Ferguson, 1994).

One such struggle concerns the challenge posed to dominant (masculine/managerialist) discourses of accountability, power and control by feminine discourses which place emphasis on cooperation, empowerment and 'people' skills – discourses that form the basis of (pro) women's voice literature discussed in the Chapter 2. In this respect, as we saw in our discussion of female advantage in contemporary organizations, the classical, 'masculine' notion of managerial work as concerned with order and control is being challenged by a 'feminine' ethos based on a recognition of the benefits of co-operation and team-working and of the need for the building of relationships and responsiveness to others (Kanter, 1989; Alvesson, 1998; Lee, 1994).

This can be seen in the primacy currently given to personal and interpersonal skills in the workplace as well as the need for imagination and creativity – attributes that have culturally been associated with femininity (e.g. Kanter, 1989; Kerfoot & Knights, 1993, 1998; Lee, 1994; Fondas, 1996, 1997; Alvesson, 1998). A recent survey by the UK-based Chartered Institute of Personnel and Development (CIPD), for example, found that customer service, client relationship and interpersonal skills were top of the list in terms of skill requirements and that interpersonal skills were the most important attributes sought in new recruits, over specialist skills or experience (CIPD, 2005). This new focus demands, in turn, a leadership style commensurate with the prioritization of relationships and with horizontal, rather than vertical, lines of communication. A more 'transformational' (Rosener, 1990) orientation to power, that is, a capacity that to empower, motivate and encourage others (discussed in detail in Chapter 2), is accordingly valorized over domination and the ability to control.

In short, competitive advantage in the marketplace is increasingly seen as dependent upon skills of cooperation and a shared influence, on the ability to build relationships with others and on the effectiveness of egalitarian partnerships both within and outside the organization. This 'feminization' of management (Fondas, 1997), so-called because it calls upon skills and attributes associated with femininity and is reflective of women's voices at work, has accordingly challenged the masculine/managerial ideal.

Suppressing the feminine and the re-emergence of masculine discourses

Challenges to the hegemonic status of ideas and values do not mean their eventual demise or replacement with alternative orientations. After all, trends towards the feminization of management outlined above have not led to significant increases in women in top managerial positions or to identifiable reductions in the problems they face. Feminine discourses, while infiltrating some organizational priorities, have not been able to significantly shift dominant masculine attitudes, values or behaviours. Instead, through rhetoric strategies and the repositioning of some behaviours, dominant discourses may suppress alternative meanings and so 'fight off' challenges to their prevailing position (Collinson & Collinson, 1996; Metcalfe & Linstead, 2003). In fact, as Calas and Smircich (1992) argue, rather than challenging the hegemonic status, feminization of management literature may serve to reinforce masculine discourses because feminine subjectivities and meanings that underpin such trends are themselves constructed under patriarchy. As such, they are diminished and devalued and so easily put aside or ignored, thereby giving space to a legitimization of dominant ideas.

Metcalfe and Linstead's (2003) study of team-working is a case in point. While team-working is ostensibly based on collaborative and supportive work attitudes and relations commonly labelled female, Metcalfe and Linstead uncovered dominant and traditional masculinist discourses of control and a performance (masculine) rhetoric around achievement, purpose, accountability and goals. Despite the encouragement of interpersonal ('feminine') skills, such as effective communication, constructive conflict, active listening, helpful criticism and mutual support, these were rarely recognized as feminine and were subsumed under masculine discourses of efficiency and output. At the same time, female-oriented team relations and processes, while integral to effective team-working, became a potential arena for instrumental control – to be captured or harnessed to achieve the end of maximum performance potential (this similar to Fletcher's (1994) argument, discussed in Chapter 2, concerning the instrumental use to which 'feminine' attributes have been put). These discourses effectively subjugated and suppressed values and practices associated with femaleness and femininity.

As Metcalfe and Linstead point out:

> Feminine qualities and sensibilities are not named as such, rather, there are hints of feminization, within, and under, patriarchal discourses of performance. Supportive, consensual and collaborative behaviours are to be encouraged . . . . . . but always in the context of improving performance'. (104)

Furthermore:

> The subtext in team discourses reveals how team output is associated with masculinity and performance, what a team achieves is above all the most significant aspect of understanding teams and team working. Significantly, team behaviours and attitudes must demonstrate commitment to achievement and control, and deny any possibilities for closer intimacy. Team theorising language is thus imbued with imagery of maleness and of constructing male identity work'. (105)

Women's voices are thus 'engulfed' in descriptions of teamwork constructed around a masculinist discourse that carries latent meanings reflective of gender relations of domination and subordination. Therefore, as Metcalfe and Linstead argue, attempts to introduce 'feminine capital' may not destabilize masculine cultural norms, but through managerial and institutional arrangements, further reinforce patriarchal power relations.

Similarly, Alvesson's (1998) study of gender relations in an advertising agency demonstrates how, within a 'feminized' environment, masculinity can maintain and re-establish its hegemonic status. Here, the culture and much of the work could be seen as 'feminine'. The (female-oriented) metaphor of the family was commonly drawn upon by staff to highlight the closeness of relationships, the role of team-working and the importance placed on emotionality (e.g. the need for sensitivity towards others). The work involved imagination and creativity, culturally associated with femininity (Hines, 1992; Fondas, 1997) and there was a 'feminine' concern with customer relations and customer care. On the face of it, this seems a far cry from rational, bureaucratic 'masculine' forms of organizing.

However, within this 'feminized' context, hierarchical gender relations were reproduced and maintained. In its starkest terms, this could be seen in the gendered division of labour whereby project assistants were female and project managers all male. Women's subordinate position was further underscored by a focus, on the part of men, on the sexual attractiveness of female recruits and by a language of sexism (e.g. via jokes and innuendo) which referred to female staff in an objectifying and degrading way. As Alvesson argues, the 'feminine' ethos of the agency posed a challenge to masculine identities. Through their language, attitudes and behaviour (i.e. through discourse), men attempted to repair and support a 'damaged' masculinity by highlighting workplace sexuality and subjecting female staff to a 'hyper-feminization' that confined them to a belittling, sexualized role. Male power was thus reasserted through masculine discourses which legitimized the controlling 'male gaze' of women and through a gendered and sexualized division of labour which entailed the recruitment of younger sexually attractive women to subordinate positions.

Both these studies demonstrate how feminine discourses, while gaining ground in some organizational contexts, are rarely hegemonic in the sense that they represent dominant ways of thinking and doing. While 'feminine' practices, such as team-working, are increasingly encouraged, masculine discourses can re-emerge through rhetoric and practices that place emphasis on performance, commitment and control.

Silencing through discourse

Dominant ways of thinking and seeing can therefore be the site of struggle as alternative orientations challenge their hegemonic status. As part of this struggle, discourses can imbue 'Other' ideas as dangerous, can discredit or render ridiculous their meanings or can silence the voices concerned. For example, the rise of the Suffragette movement at the turn of the twenty-first century led to a discourse of danger and disruption, with strong rhetoric around predictions of the downfall of empire and the fabric of society.

> Unless those who hold that the success of the women's suffrage movement would bring disaster upon England are prepared to take immediate and effective action, judgement may go by default and our country drift towards a momentous revolution both social and political before it realises the dangers involved. Women's National Anti-suffrage League Manifesto, (1909) cited in Marlow (2000: 80)

More recently, dominant and powerful discourses of racism and multiculturalism have also successfully silenced issues of sexism associated with particular racial and religious groups – or have relabelled and neutralized such concerns under a rhetoric of 'culture' and 'tradition'.

Silence and silencing are further responses to actual or potential challenges from dominant ideas. In this respect, Fondas (1997) found a rhetoric of 'feminization' in her study of management texts, whereby 'feminine' qualities and attributes were increasingly recognized by writers on management as beneficial. However, in a similar vein to Metcalfe and Linstead (2003) above, they were rarely named or recognized as such. In other words, while the *qualities* of the feminine may be given priority there was a silence around the *associations with the feminine*. As Fondas (1997) argues, this reflects the problematic meanings attached to the feminine in a culture based on binary opposites of masculine and feminine – where the latter is denigrated and the former given priority:

> feminine words and names are problematic signifiers for management writers whose audience is predominantly male managers. They hear terms such as *soft* to mean *not hard*, *connected* to mean *not independent*, *helping others* to mean *not achieving individually*, and *surrendering* to mean *not victorious*. What they hear reflects the culture's unconscious practice of sexual asymmetry, particularly its denigration of the feminine'. Fondas (1997: 273, author's italics)

As Fondas argues, by scrutinizing the language in texts, one can hear not only what is being said but also what is being silenced – in this case all associations with women or with femininity. The benefits of 'feminine' ways of organizing are recognized – but not named as such.

In a study of the construction of sexual identities in the workplace and the silence that often greeted the 'coming out' (disclosure of sexual orientation) of sexual minorities at work, Ward and Winstanley (2003) point out that naming is an important form of social acknowledgement. Lack of naming can therefore comprise a 'blankness' or 'rubbing out', keeping individuals concerned invisible and hence making it difficult for them to construct their (in this case 'out') identities. On this basis, an absence of response, as a frequent reaction to 'coming out' of colleagues at work, could be seen as a 'powerful presence'. Silencing was used by the dominant group as an active means of 'Othering' sexual minorities, so suppressing their identities as individuals and as a group.

Refusal to name can therefore suppress or fail to give credence to alternative views, and identities. Other forms of silencing can also occur – particularly over issues that may intrude upon or disrupt the 'ideal' functioning of organizations (Acker, 1990). For example, Mills (2002) suggests that a silence can exist in organizations around 'female' areas of sexuality, emotions and discriminatory practices while Martin (1990) points out there is often a silence around conflict as dominant ideologies deny the existence of points of view that could be disruptive of existing power relations. This can be seen in the way prevailing normative rules marginalize and suppress sexual harassment as an issue worthy of consideration and debate (Collinson & Collinson, 1996; Wilson & Thompson, 2001). Women's interests accordingly appear as contradictions and disruptions – or as silences.

Silence can therefore play an important role in organizational discourse as well as in the creation of social identity. As Gabriel et al. (2000) point out, meanings and assumptions created by a discursive regime are inevitably based on omissions and evasions. As we have seen in the examples above, by foregrounding and privileging some interpretations, others are silenced as unsuitable or excessive. In this respect, and in a similar vein to Ward and Winstanley (2003) above, Calas and Smirich (1999) point to the salience of 'presence' and 'absence'. In this context, the unexpressed can be seen to constitute text as absence and silence makes possible the placement of limits or containments on what is said and enables that meaning to appear. In other words, representations depend on a silent/invisible and/or devalued 'Other' for legitimation.

For example, as Ward and Winstanley argue, hegemonic discourse is based on the implicit rule that precludes open discussion of the experiences of marginalized people. Heterosexuality retains its dominant status because of its refusal to recognize or give credence to alternative identities and meanings. Similarly, masculinity retains its status because it silences, through a refusal to name, any valorization of the (devalued) feminine, even though it may recognize the benefits of some of the associated qualities. Dominant discourses may therefore *silence* oppositional meanings or may *contain them* by allowing them some limited and devalued space (Fairclough, 1989). Silence is therefore present in the discourse, either as an absence or as a devalued presence, and helps to construct its meaning. In this way, heterosexuality is constructed on a (silent and/or devalued) Other of homosexuality; masculinity is constructed on a (silent and/or devalued) Other of femininity.

There is accordingly a hierarchical arrangement based on that which is said (presence) and what is unsaid (absence). Meaning is thereby constituted within a system of power relations – a system of inclusion and exclusion and of presence and absence – which defines knowledge. In this way, as Foucault (1976) suggests, silence constitutes discourse and can be an agent of power in its own right in that silence contains the taboo or the forbidden. Therefore, to understand discourse, it needs to be 'pieced together, with things both said and unsaid, with required and with forbidden speech' (Foucault, 1976: 133 cited in Ward & Winstanley, 2003: 1260).

Power relations are therefore predicated on silences – and discourses can be seen as part of a process that creates and maintains that silence. As Martin (1990) suggests, it is in these 'spaces' that the presence of ideology can be most positively felt and where ideological assumptions particularly sensitive to the suppressed interests of marginalized groups can be uncovered. By adopting the deeper conceptualization of 'voice', which goes further than seeing voice as a state of absence or neglect, we can explore the processes that serve to maintain silence and the significance of the 'silent space'.

Conclusion

In this chapter we have moved away from the liberal and radical feminist inspired 'women's voice' perspective associated with surface conceptualizations which, as we saw in Chapter 2, are grounded in the recognition of gender difference and the need to listen to women's accounts of their experiences. This orientation accordingly sees 'lack of voice' as a *state of absence and neglect*. In this chapter we have highlighted, at a 'deeper' level, how this fails to address the *process of silencing* that occurs, which helps to demonstrate why some voices are dominant while others continue to go unheard.

In this context, from a post-structuralist perspective, we have drawn more fundamentally on the concept of 'discourse' (as signs, labels, expressions and rhetoric) which shape our thinking, attitudes and behaviour and, by creating meanings, help to frame our concepts of 'normality' as well as our sense of self. Through our analysis of the discourses of managerialism and masculinity, we have shown how dominant discourses can underpin and support each other, as well as some of the challenges (e.g. in the form of the feminization of management discourse) they have faced. To maintain their hegemonic status, dominant discourses need to 'fight off' such challenges. Accordingly, dominant ways of thinking and seeing, underpinned by an appropriate language, enable voices which support these meanings to be heard while other, dissenting voices are silenced – as excessive, ridiculous or unreasonable. In order to appreciate why, at a surface level, women's voices have gone unheard we need to draw on (deep) understandings of the power of dominant discourses in conveying appropriate meanings, and of the role of silence in dominant discursive regimes.

4

Visibility: a surface state of exclusion and difference

Introduction

Boston ambush

A recent report in *The Guardian* (11 July 2003) tells the story of Reggie Cummings, a black software developer, who got tired of being the only black face in bars and restaurants in town after dark. He contacted every local black professional group in the area and, in a 'friendly take-over' of clubs and bars, arranged to email them with the latest venue to get 'a little colour' into the night-time Boston scene. Before this attempt at greater integration, local black men and women spoke of feeling 'uncomfortable' as the only (or one of a few) black person present. As one lawyer commented:

> White people in the US have had their comfort zones all their lives – they don't have to go looking for it. It's always interesting to me to observe even the most positive, forward thinking progressive member of the majority culture when they are surrounded by minorities. All of a sudden they have to struggle with the fact that they are now a minority. But that is what most black people in the US have to deal with all the time.

This story is about visibility and the problems of 'standing out in the crowd'. Walking into a crowded bar and being the only back face means you are highly visible and this can lead to feelings of being out of place and of discomfort. It is also a story about how members of the numerical minority are made to embody difference (race) while the majority represent the universal (white) case. When the tables are turned, and the majority become outnumbered, they too experience discomfort and become aware of *their* difference.

In the context of gender, this chapter looks at the problems of visibility. The increase in the participation of women in the labour market in the post-war period and their growing infiltration into what had previously been male-only occupations and professions has contributed to a growing interest in what happens when women begin to occupy jobs that have been previously the exclusive domain of men. What are the group dynamics when a small number of people in a particular category are introduced into a much larger group? What sort of problems do they encounter and how do they respond? Such work, rather than focusing on *individual* attributes (e.g. skills and qualifications) as in the women's voice perspective outlined in the last chapter, has placed emphasis on the *structures* of the organization in the form of group size and composition. In particular, the focus has been on how they influence attitudes and behaviours at work.

These structures are important because people tend to identify themselves with groups and these groups affect how people behave. The basis for group formation will depend on the context but, as Byrne (1971) has argued, individuals are likely to be attracted to others who are similar to themselves. An easily identifiable and visible characteristic such as age, sex and race can, as we saw in the case of Reggie Cummings above, be used as a basis of group membership and so help define boundaries between 'insiders' and 'outsiders'. The implications of heightened visibility associated with categorization and minority status within the group forms the basis of much research in this area. Such work has therefore explored the material consequences for the minority group (usually women) as they enter male-dominated occupations and become highly visible in that they 'stand out in the crowd'.

This chapter on visibility focuses on 'surface' states of *exclusion and difference* that run through much of the broadly liberal feminist work on the implications of 'token' status. At this surface level, visibility is seen as a numerically burdensome state. There is therefore little regard for deeper processes that keep some issues hidden from view – issues that are explored in the next chapter. A key concept here is difference. However, while in women's voice literature difference refers to *differences between* groups (male/female), in this literature the key focus is on the consequences of *difference from* the majority group. One therefore charts variations between men and women while the other focuses on the consequences (usually for women) of being noticeable, conspicuous, in full view.

Much of the work on visibility has focused on the problems that arise as women enter male-dominated organizations and occupations. Kanter's (1977) study of an American corporation, Indsco is foundational in this respect. Drawing on earlier work by Blau (1970, 1977), Kanter developed a structural analysis of the implications of the sex composition of groups. Both Kanter and Blau were concerned with the impact of group size on inter and intra-group relations. Their analyses rest on two assumptions: that increased rates of social interaction among individuals will lead to the formation of affective ties to members of a given social group and that such ties affect individual's attitudes to the group. According to Blau, men and women in work organizations are more likely to interact with each other if they are in the same rather than different work groups and the amount of interaction is likely to increase when work groups are mixed. This in turn will improve the quality of inter-group relations (i.e. relations between men and women). If tokens experience negative attitudes and practices, this is due to the low opportunity of the group's majority members to interact with a token minority members and so to develop attitudes of acceptance towards that group.

Building on this work, Kanter explored the dynamics of asymmetric groups within her case study corporation. Her focus here was on the implications of visibility and difference for relations between the groups and for the subjective state of members of the minority. In particular, she emphasized the way in which the proportion of individuals in a work setting with a particular visible characteristic (e.g. sex) affects that characteristic's salience within the group and so how the numerically dominant behave towards the minority.

Kanter proposed four types of groups dependent on the ratios of the numerically dominant to the numerical minority. Of interest here is the 'skewed' group where the ratio is about 85:15 and where members of the minority are referred to as 'tokens'. Tokens experience three processes which are detrimental to their experiences within the organization and to their careers. High *visibility* creates increased performance pressures; *polarization* occurs as differences between the dominant group and tokens are exaggerated leading to separation and isolation; finally *assimilation* occurs as individuals are made to fit into stereotypical roles associated with their (minority) group. Core to each process is the consequences of difference associated with high visibility.

High visibility can have negative consequences for the minority group. Tokens are often marginalized, judged negatively and forced into stereotypical roles. As Simpson (1997, 2000) found in a study of women managers, gender imbalance and associated visibility heightens career barriers, limits career progress and helps to create a hostile working environment for the minority (female) group.

According to Kanter, the majority becomes sensitized to the visible characteristic that identifies the minority status of the token. In terms of gender, men use this visible difference to construct boundaries between the majority male and minority female groups. Men choose people most like themselves for friendships, networks, teams, promotions – a process referred to as 'homosociablility'. This sets the scene for the marginalization and exclusion of women. These social boundaries promote interaction among majority members and minimizes contact with minorities. In other words, an easily visible demographic characteristic such as age, sex and race is used as an index of similarity so tokens are seen as representatives of their category or as symbols rather than as individuals. The numerically dominant accordingly suffer from 'perceptual distortions' regarding tokens' characteristics and actions, so that tokens suffer the burden of representing their category rather than having their performance taken at face value.

In this respect, women in management stand out because they are unusual. High visibility means they get attention and their abilities are often eclipsed by their physical appearance. As Kanter pointed out, women often dress conservatively in order to reduce visibility and to avoid being seen as sexual beings. Visibility can lead to performance pressures because nearly everything they do is noticed. As Marshall (1994) and Maddock (1999) found, women are often given difficult tasks as a performance test, leading to extra pressure not to make mistakes (Kanter, 1977; Powney, 1997; Cross & Bagilhole, 2002b). At the same time, women may attempt to reduce visibility and gain acceptance by becoming 'one of the boys' – behaving and working like men.

Polarization

As we have seen, 'homosocialibity', whereby men choose others most like themselves, leads to the drawing of boundaries along gendered lines. This promotes interaction among majority members and minimizes contact with minorities. Through the resulting segregation, the dominant group becomes highly aware of what makes them dominant so making more visible the differences between them – a process referred to as 'polarization'. The commonality of members of the dominant group is brought home to them by the visible presence of tokens, helping to exaggerate their contrasting characteristics and heighten group boundaries. According to Kanter, men are likely to behave in more 'masculine' ways in the presence of women, so tokens serve to underline the dominant culture – a culture tokens must accept as they are too few in number to be influential in this respect. 'Macho' behaviour may accordingly intensify as more women enter the organization and so become a greater threat to men (Zimmer, 1988) and as men become territorial about 'their' occupations (Williams, 1993) or resent the intrusion of women and the unwelcome competition (Cross & Bagilhole, 2002b).

Furthermore, as Kanter observed, token women performed the function of audience to the 'dominant cultural expression' of men. Men's sense of camaraderie deepened in their presence. They dramatized and acted out masculinity more fervently in the company of token women than when they were in an all male group: they regaled each other with tales of sexual adventure, told off-colour jokes and took part in heavy drinking. Other studies suggest, in a similar vein, that aggressive behaviour is more evident and sexuality more prominent and more problematic for women in work contexts that are numerically male dominated (Ely, 1994; Cross & Bagilhole, 2002a). In the priesthood, for example, women have referred to the 'aggressive', 'brutish' and bullying behaviour of male colleagues (Cross & Bagilhole, 2002b) while sexual harassment has been found to be more prevalent when women are in the minority (Cockburn, 1991; Collinson & Collinson, 1996). Homosociability, the need to assert the dominant masculine culture as well as feelings of threat to female entrants, can therefore exaggerate perceptions of differences between the dominant and minority group and lead to a polarization between the two.

Assimilation

Kanter identified four 'role traps' which form around perceptions of a particular behavioural tendency on the part of tokens. This is then exaggerated and built into an image of the token's role in the group. Assimilation occurs when tokens are forced to conform to these roles. All subsequent behaviour is interpreted in terms of that role. The 'mother' role is based on a stereotype of a woman as a good listener, sympathetic, an emotional specialist who is rewarded for services to others rather than for independent action. The 'seductress' is a sexually charged and a more dangerous role because of the possibility of arousing jealousy and retaliation. The 'pet' role sees women as cute, amusing, not particularly sexual – and 'cheering from the sidelines' rather than instigating independent action. If a token refuses to accept these roles, then she becomes an 'iron maiden' – sexless, 'school-mistressy' and an object of ridicule by the rest of the group. High visibility therefore forces women into one of these stereotypical role traps. Each one is a constraint on independent action. The dynamics of role entrapment, for example, can lead tokens to a variety of conservative or low risk behaviours in order to reduce visibility and the likelihood of being pressurized into one particular undesirable role.

Responses of tokens to high visibility

As Kanter argues, tokens experience a number of contradictions and pressures. They are both representative and exceptions. They are made aware of their difference but must pretend the differences don't exist. They are highly visible but at the same time are marginalized in a masculine culture which devalues the feminine. They can be made to fit into stereotypical roles associated with their group (seductress, mother, pet, iron maiden) constraining behaviour so as to fit the 'role trap'.

So how do tokens respond to this situation? According to Kanter, tokens can be afraid to be too outstanding in performance in group events. This fear of success can occur if the retaliation costs of succeeding in an alien environment are seen to be too high. Tokens would then try to make themselves invisible – such as avoiding conflict or being reluctant to speak at meetings. Women may also opt to keep a low profile to avoid role entrapment and to prevent hostile reactions from men. Few women, for example, report incidents of sexual harassment because of a fear of retaliation and ridicule – as well as a need to protect their professional interests in a context where such complaints are often not taken seriously (Collinson & Collinson, 1996).

A further response may be for women to behave like men. Here tokens succeed but do so by being 'one of the boys' and by disassociating themselves from the minority group to which they really belong. In Ely's (1994) study, female lawyers often perceived the characteristics ascribed to women as a liability in their firms while in the Civil Service, Cross and Bagilhole (2002b) found that women felt they needed to be aggressive, pushy and dominating to succeed. In both studies, women tried to distance themselves from 'femininity' and tended to model themselves on men – and to adopt values and behaviours traditionally associated with masculinity. This has been referred to as the Queen Bee syndrome (Kanter, 1977) and may result in women becoming highly ambitious and single-minded in the pursuit of their careers. Women in this position often deny the salience of gender in their careers choices and experiences (Rubin, 1997), claiming to have relied on their own resources and efforts to succeed. In denying the existence of discrimination, queen bees are unlikely to support other women in the organization and often blame them for their lack of achievement. Being 'one of the boys' and failing to help or be sympathetic to other women was a frequent response, according to Kanter, to a token's position within a dominant group – though being too manly could attract criticism and the 'iron maiden' label.

In summary, Kanter and other authors in the field have identified a number of social behaviours exhibited by majority members which are associated with the high visibility of members of the numerically minority group: increased solidarity in response to the heightened salience of their common group awareness; close scrutiny of the behaviour and performance of individual minority members; and cross group interactions characterized by the role casting of minorities in ways consistent with common cultural stereotypes. Kanter hypothesized that as a result of the implications of high visibility, minority members would experience psychological pressures associated with a growing sense of social isolation, intense performance pressure and unusually strong social constraints on their behaviour in social interactions. Tokens are accordingly likely to respond in ways that help to reduce the effects of visibility – from keeping a low profile to attempts to become assimilated into the world of men.

A question of numbers: the benefits of sex integration

The work on numerical asymmetry is based on the assumption that the negative effects that accrue to individuals in underrepresented groups will be vastly reduced or eliminated once balanced representation is achieved. As a 'critical mass' is achieved (e.g. as more black men and women enter white-dominated clubs and bars), there would be a greater level of interaction with and acceptance by the dominant group (Blau, 1977; Kanter, 1977). In the context of gender, as the proportion of women in senior positions increases, the negative consequences of visibility are reduced and the experiences of all women in the organization would consequently improve. In fact, according to the 'pipeline' theory (Dobson, 1997), this balance will occur over time as more women enter the workforce and eventually proceed along the 'pipeline' into senior management. But how will numbers alone facilitate this move towards gender equality? There are several possibilities here.

By creating a counter culture that is less aggressive and competitive, the dominant culture can become less hostile and more cooperative and accepting of others. Homosociability (whereby men choose others like themselves) may become less powerful and so open the doors for more women. Equalizing groups may also help reduce perceptual distortions and so encourage the dominant group to see members of the minority as individuals rather than as representatives of their category. Sexuality, for example, may become less salient as the number of women in senior positions increases – so reducing the likelihood of role entrapment and negative stereotyping. As Kanter stated:

> Organizations with a better balance of people would be more tolerant of the differences among them. In addition to making affirmative action a reality there would be other benefits: a reduction in stress on the people who are 'different', a reduction in the conformity pressure of the dominant group. It would be more possible in such an organization to build the skill and utilize the competence of people who currently operate at a disadvantage. (1977: 283–284)

Once in post, senior women may act as mentors, sponsors and role models for others lower down the organizational hierarchy, heightening career aspirations as well as helping to create a more woman-friendly environment (though as we have seen, queen bees may not act in this way!). Femininity may be less likely to be devalued in more sex integrated organizations. As Ely (1994) points out, women in numerically balanced work contexts draw on both traditionally masculine and feminine images and portray femininity in positive ways. Women can therefore be aggressive and forthright but also relate empathetically to colleagues and clients. In other words, a wider range of behaviours (by women) are viewed more positively when women have greater numerical representation in the organization.

Reduced visibility: can numbers lead to gender equality?

This previous section suggests that an increase in numbers shifts the group dynamics and reduces the visibility of the minority group. This reduces feelings of psychological discomfort and stress, largely the outcome of heightened visibility and the negative environment created by the majority's attitudes and behaviours. The culture of the organization becomes more accepting of the minority group, homosociability and its effects are diminished and equality becomes within reach. There are, however, a number of problems associated with this rather optimistic scenario.

Some work has suggested that, rather than laying the foundations for greater equality, an increase in numbers may actually exacerbate negative consequences of minority status. Bagilhole (2002) for example, found in a study of the construction industry that tensions and hostilities increased as more women entered the occupation. As Zimmer (1988) has argued, negative effects of tokenism may intensify as women increase in number because they present a greater threat to men. As argued earlier, men may become more territorial about 'their' occupations (Williams, 1993) and resent the unwelcome competition (Cross & Bagilhole, 2002a). They may also fear a 'feminization' of the occupation and the consequent challenge to masculine identities (Cockburn, 1985, 1991; Cross & Bagilhole, 2002a) – identities that are often founded on the work environment (Morgan, 1992). Furthermore, as Ely (1994) argues, it is not just the quantity of women but the position that they hold in the hierarchy that is important. If there is an absence of women at the top, difficulties will persist for women lower down the hierarchy despite a balanced representation at those levels.

More fundamentally, however, these explanations fail to recognize the complexities of male advantage, gender power and the gendered nature of organizational dynamics (Zimmer, 1988; Alvesson & Due Billing, 1992). Kanter (1977), for example, in identifying numbers as the primary cause of the negative effects encountered by members of the minority, neglects the impact of differences in status or gender. According to Kanter, a proportional increase in the representation of the minority group, whatever their basis (e.g. gender, race), will be sufficient to reduce the negative processes of tokenism. Therefore, the reason women experience particular problems in management positions is not because they are women but because they are numerically in the minority and so visible and subject to surveillance and scrutiny. As women achieve 'critical mass' by entering organizations, disadvantages will disappear.

In accordance with liberal feminism, 'tokenism' and associated organizational structures are taken to be gender neutral. However, this overlooks the gender bias within those structures and how they reflect and are reinforced by broader structural and cultural inequalities. In other words, these accounts neglect the potential-mediating impact of general social prestige and status accorded to different groups in society (Yoder, 1991, 1994) Therefore, numbers alone cannot create equality because of other social and cultural factors which privilege the masculine and devalue the feminine (Zimmer, 1988; Heikes, 1992). So, while Kanter claims that the pressures described above would apply to any minority group irrespective of its characterization or composition, such that there would be little if any difference between the experiences of male and female tokens, other research has indicated that women in the minority have more undesirable social experiences than men (e.g. Heikes, 1992; Konrad et al., 1992) – because of traditional gender roles which label the workplace a masculine domain.

Visibility and the dynamics of asymmetric groups: the male advantage?

Kanter and other works on the dynamics of asymmetric groups (e.g. Blau, 1977) predict that men in subgroups would experience the same sorts of negative psychological outcomes of high visibility as women – in the form, for example, of social isolation and heightened performance pressures. However, if organizational structures can be seen to be fundamentally gendered, then it would be reasonable to suppose that outcomes for men in female-dominated occupations might be different. In other words, visibility may have different career and psychological implications from those encountered by women.

Perhaps in response to the increased number of men who have been recently entering female-dominated occupations, a growing body of research (e.g. Heikes, 1992; Williams, 1993; Simpson, 2004) has been exploring their career progress and experiences in the organization. This work suggests that while 'token' women can be severely disadvantaged by their minority status, assumptions of male careerism and managerial potential often mean positive career outcomes accruing for men (Floge & Merril, 1986). Men working in non-traditional occupations have been found to benefit from their token status through the assumption of enhanced leadership and other skills and by being associated with a more careerist attitude to work (Floge & Merril, 1986; Heikes, 1992). Male nurses often ascend the hierarchy more quickly than female counterparts (Bradley, 1993). Men therefore tend to monopolize positions of power and are rewarded for their difference from women in terms of higher pay and other benefits (Williams, 1993).

Heightened visibility, which is seen to adversely affect the performance of token women, may be advantageous for men. As Simpson (2004) found, men in primary school teaching were often asked to take charge of difficult or demanding situations (e.g. giving advice, taking the lead at meetings, dealing with difficult situations) commensurate with an authority ascribed to a masculine status. In nursing men were frequently given 'first crack of the whip' in terms of access to training or developmental opportunities (such as attending operations). Rather than leading to highly cautious behaviour, as Kanter predicted in her study of women, Simpson suggests that visibility and assumptions of authority may well be developmental for men by exposing them to challenging situations that demand initiative and resourcefulness. As Heikes (1992) found, in his study of male nurses, men reacted to visibility by over achieving. Most men viewed their visibility in a positive light since it often led to special consideration by managers and brought their competence and skills to the attention of others.

Special consideration afforded to male nurses on the ward

Simpson (2005) cites the case of a male nurse who committed the 'cardinal sin' of being late for duty – a situation that would normally demand a reprimand from the nurse in charge:

> On one particular occasion I overslept for an early shift and I was woken in the nurses' home by somebody hammering on my door at nine thirty to say the ward's on the phone. So I went to the phone and it was the sister saying 'You've overslept'. And I said 'Yes, I'm ever so sorry'. And she was going 'No, no, not a problem, have you had your breakfast?' 'No, I haven't had breakfast'. 'Well you get your breakfast inside you and then you make your way up to work and don't worry we'll see you when you get here'. So I got ready, had my breakfast, sauntered up to the hospital and got onto the ward about eleven o'clock.'

As this nurse subsequently admitted, his female colleagues would not have been treated in such a lenient way!

Two further conditions (polarization and assimilation) were thought by Kanter to disadvantage members of minority groups. As we have seen, polarization refers to the isolation and marginalization of tokens by the dominant group where it is the *dominant group* that engages in boundary heightening. Studies of men in non-traditional occupations (e.g. Heikes, 1992; Cross & Bagilhole, 2002a; Simpson, 2004, 2005), however, suggest that it is often the *minority of men* who attempt to separate themselves from the female majority. Distance was therefore created by men as they sought to separate themselves from women and the 'female' associations of the job. In other words, when tokens are of a higher status, they may attempt to differentiate themselves from lower status dominants. In this case it is the minority that raise boundaries to the dominant group.

The third condition discussed by Kanter – assimilation – refers to how individuals, made visible by their minority status, are assumed to take on the stereotypical characteristics of their group and so be confined to corresponding 'role traps'. Some evidence of stereotypical roles has emerged from other studies of men (Heikes, 1992; Simpson, 2004). In Simpson's study of primary school teacher, nurses and cabin crew, men were given a 'father' role. They were expected to be the disciplinarian, to take charge of demanding situations and to be authoritative in formal work settings while younger men could find themselves in a 'son' role – looked after by older female staff.

As Simpson (2004, 2005) suggests, outcomes of assimilation may be less detrimental than in Kanter's analysis. First, men may not be trapped in their roles to the same extent as women, who often encounter sanctions if they do not conform to type. Instead, men have greater integrity over choice of behaviours, that is, they can choose whether or not to conform to the role. Secondly, rather than being confining or belittling, father or son roles may be developmental through exposure to learning opportunities. Therefore, contrary to the predictions of Kanter, who saw the disadvantages of token status as applying to all minority groups, men may well benefit from preferential treatment and from exposure to roles and situations that are challenging and developmental. This suggests, in accordance with Bradley (1993) and Heikes (1992), a need to include social and cultural factors into any analysis of the structural significance of numbers. A focus on numbers alone, as in Kanter's work, overlooks the positive cultural valuation given to male attributes in society and the rewards which accordingly accrue.

Conclusion

In this chapter we have explored the gender literature on visibility. As with the surface conceptualization of voice considered in the Chapter 2, work on 'surface' visibility is concerned with states of inequality whereby certain groups are not fully accepted or recognized. Here, visibility is to be different and disadvantaged. In other words, to be visible is to 'stand out in the crowd' – to be seen as different and hence to be isolated and marginalized from the dominant group.

Work in this area (e.g. Kanter, 1977; Heikes, 1992; Ely, 1994; Simpson, 1997, 2000) therefore views visibility as a numerical (and often burdensome) state whereby individuals are made to embody their difference and conform to stereotypical roles. Heightened visibility means women can be subject to increased performance pressures while a desire for invisibility can manifest itself in a fear of success, low- risk behaviour and/or avoidance of conflict. Alternatively, women may behave like men in an attempt to become assimilated into the majority group.

However, while visibility and 'token' status have been found to be detrimental and burdensome for women, men in token positions may be able to draw on the privileges of their sex. As we have seen, men working in female-dominated occupations can benefit from their token status through the assumption of enhanced leadership and other skills and by being associated with a more careerist attitude to work (Floge & Merril, 1986; Heikes, 1992; Williams, 1993). They tend to monopolize positions of power and are often rewarded for their difference from women in terms of higher pay and other benefits (Williams, 1993). This difference is often underpinned by a tendency, on the part of men, to distance themselves from the female colleagues and from female associations of the job (Lupton, 2000; Simpson, 2004). Therefore, while outcomes of token status may vary by gender, in both cases visibility is associated with *difference and a state of exclusion*, whether through choice (men) or through coercion (women), from the dominant group.

Some overlaps and differences exist between surface conceptualizations of voice (discussed in Chapter 2) and visibility. Both literatures have liberal feminist orientations (though women's voice as we have seen includes radical feminist elements) and conceive of gender as stable categories based on characteristics which are either inherent or acquired through socialization. Both focus on 'gender justice' and the need to reform rather than transform existing structures. Thus, equality initiatives would allow women's voices to be heard and their experiences and needs to be incorporated into the organization. Equally, problems of visibility would dissipate once women were no longer organizational minorities.

Literature in each area focuses on a state of inequality. 'Voice' incorporates neglect and a failure to include female perspectives and experiences while 'visibility' is largely concerned with the consequences of difference for the minority group. At this surface level, voice therefore is oriented towards seeing inequality as a state of absence and neglect based on the 'weak presence' of women while with visibility inequality is viewed as a state of exclusion and difference. One therefore demands that we listen to women and hear their accounts and experiences and has an orientation towards *differences between* men and women, while the other explores material consequences of the sex structuring of organizations and *difference from* (as in heightened visibility) the dominant group.

Both are concerned with inequality as *states* – thereby ignoring deeper processes of silencing (discussed in Chapter 3) or processes which help to keep issues hidden from view. Therefore, while work on 'token' status seeks to demonstrate the material consequences of visibility, it does not question in any substantial way the privileging and invisibility of the norm against which women and other minorities are often measured. As the black lawyer in the Boston Ambush story presented at the start of this chapter intimated, whites are invisible as a racial group – their whiteness hidden within the norm. Only when they are outnumbered by blacks do they have to confront their (racial) difference. This suggests a need to focus on deeper phenomenon than 'surface states' of exclusion and difference – and to explore the invisibility and dynamics of the norm and the implications for those both inside and outside its domain. This forms the subject matter of the next chapter.

5

Deep conceptualizations of invisibility

Introduction

This chapter explores deep conceptualizations of invisibility. In particular it considers the implications of belonging to the advantaged gender group of men, where a significant part of the privilege attached to being a man is the ability not to think about gender at all, not to take any notice whatsoever of its role in daily life. As briefly discussed in Chapter 1, men have retained their power partly because they are considered the normative standard case – as such they are invisible to analysis and the privileges attendant on their gender often go unnoticed. However, the strength of discourses around equality and the greater visibility afforded to male privilege through this discourse has led to counterclaims of disadvantage by men. The notion that men are increasingly experiencing disadvantage is becoming well established (Burke & Black 1997; Leck, 2002) and in this respect the chapter will reflect on the subject of the 'male backlash'. Men's quest for visibility as 'victims' and its association with their privileged invisible status will be explored. It will be argued that a significant impact of men's claim to the identity of victim is to reinforce the advantage gained from men's invisible association with a universalized norm.

Man – the invisible gender(less) subject

A key focus of organizational writing throughout the twentieth century has been the phenomenon of 'men at work'. In classic texts such as *Men who Manage* (Dalton, 1959) and the *Organization Man* (Whyte, 1956) men are put at the centre of considerations of management and organizations but are not themselves the target of analysis. Men's pervasive presence in organization texts appears to give their dominance a universality that prohibits the need for further analysis. Categories such as workers, managers, bureaucrats, entrepreneurs are used interchangeably with 'men' (Collinson & Hearn, 1996). Thus while the subject of much organizational writing about organizations, managers and management is de facto a man, the impact of gender on his experience of all facets of organizational life is regularly ignored. Men as managers tend to be viewed as genderless, with most men not realizing that they have a gender which affects their working lives. This was clearly demonstrated by Whitehead (2001b: 77) when he asked 24 male education managers whether gender had been a factor in their career progression. He found that most of the men were puzzled and had little idea of what the question meant – as illustrated by some of their responses:

> Mmm . . . interesting, can you expand on that to help me out?
> I don't know . . . I really don't know how I could answer that
> That is difficult. Difficult to give you a realistic answer . . . I'm not a woman
> No idea . . . I can't answer that question
> I've never thought about it; I don't treat women differently
> No I'm lucky, I've always worked with men
> Oh God! I don't know . . . I've always tried to treat men and women similarly

Two things emerge from these responses. First, respondents have some difficulty in talking about gender as an issue that has an impact on them. Secondly, gender is constructed by a number of the respondents as something which only has relevance for women (*'I'm not a woman'*). The potential to be singled out or treated differently because of gender is perceived as a concern for women and not men (*'I don't treat women differently'*).

The male respondents' view of gender as an issue or identity which they do not experience (but which women do) is reinforced in this study by the contrasting response of female respondents who had little difficulty articulating the impact of gender on their experience at work. As Whitehead argues, women cannot escape holding an active gender identity because 'like it or not, as women in these gendered organizations they had to be political. They were given little choice' (Whitehead, 2001b: 76). In other words, unlike men, women are defined by their gender. In this respect, they *have* to take up gender as an active identity while men can choose not to.

The invisible privileges of masculinity

What does this tell us about the way gender manifests itself in organizations today? It would appear that it is only when gender is a source of recognized victimization or harm that it gets noticed. We accordingly often fail to see the material and symbolic privileges of masculinity and men as a gendered phenomenon.

In this respect, we are at this stage well used to analyses of organizations which expose how membership of a disadvantaged group impacts negatively on organizational prospects. Though such analyses have benefited women through highlighting the barriers and discrimination they face, they also act to distance them from what Robinson (2000: 1) refers to as '. . . universalizing constructions of identity and narratives of experience'.

Studies of gender which only understand gender in terms of *harm* concentrate on the historically marginalized position of women and in so doing have overlooked masculinity '. . . as if it is the natural, inevitable, ordinary way of being human' (Kusz, 2001: 393). Men's pervasive dominance of the public (and private) world enables them to represent the normative standard case, universalizing their experiences and constructing their subjectivity as objective knowledge. In contrast by broadening our understanding of gender to include a consideration of the potential benefits and privileges that are derived from being a member of the advantaged gender group of men, we can expose '. . . the everyday, invisible, subtle, cultural and social practices, ideas and codes that discursively secure the power and privilege of (men) but that strategically remains unmarked, unnamed and unmapped in contemporary society' (Kusz, 2001: 393).

Commentators such as Robinson (2000), Kusz (2001) and Pierce (2003) argue that such invisibility is a necessary condition for the perpetuation of the power of advantaged groups such as men. As Robinson (2000) explains, to be invisible in this sense is not to be 'hidden from history' but rather to act as the self evident standard against which all diversity is assessed, that is, 'hidden by history'. From this perspective to be conflated with normativity assigns power both in cultural and material terms. An individual's structural position, for example, access to jobs or promotions, is heavily influenced by whether or not s/he represents the norm in any particular context.

The (invisible) resources of masculinity

Drawing on Sewell's (1992 cited in Lewis, 2004a) formulation of race as being a phenomenon which is both symbolic and structural, we can understand gender as a dual structure comprised of both cultural schemas (e.g. rules of gender interaction between men and women, understandings of differences between men and women and between the masculine and the feminine) and resources (e.g. financial wealth, cultural capital). The relationship between the material and symbolic components of gender is dialectic and as Sewell (1992: 12 cited in Lewis, 2004a: 630) suggests '.. it must be true that schemas are the effects of resources, just as resources are the effect of schemas . . . If resources are instantiations or embodiments of schemas, they therefore inculcate and justify the schemas as well . . . If schemas are to be sustained or reproduced over time . . they must be validated by the accumulation of resources that their enactment engenders'.

For example, male opposition to women's entrance into an occupation which is traditionally dominated by men is driven in part by male expectations that a female presence will lead to a decline in pay levels. Women's entrance into a traditionally dominated occupation such as pharmacy is often followed by a process referred to as 'tipping' where women's arrival is followed by the departure of men in significant numbers. While the connection between gender and pay levels is well documented and is associated with the value (or lack of value) attached to skills labelled masculine or feminine, this is a consequence of presumptions men and women draw on in making occupational choices. If men reap financial benefits from the fact that their 'skills' and characteristics consistently lead to them being paid more, this resource payoff is connected to a set of gender stereotypes. Such '. . . schemas or (gender) ideas play a key role in generating resource outcomes (e.g. higher pay levels), which in turn appear to confirm the original schemas' (Lewis, 2004a: 631).

These schemas can be understood as classificatory systems which apply a principle of difference to a population in such a way as to facilitate their division (including associated features and qualities) into at least two contrasting groups: masculine and feminine/ male and female. Social relations are produced through such classificatory systems with binary oppositions being a pervasive form of categorization (Woodward, 1997). Binary oppositions are build around notions of 'insiders' and 'outsiders' and are used to establish culturally accepted social practices.

The notion of difference which is produced through binary oppositions can be viewed positively and celebrated as a form of diversity and heterogeneity which is enriching. However, there is a difficulty with the 'celebration of difference' position in that the established components of a binary opposition are not equally valued. One element in the dichotomy is more valued or powerful than the other, '. . . often one is the norm and the other is "other" – seen as deviant or outside' leading to a power imbalance between the two. It is argued by writers such as Irigaray and de Beauvoir that these dualisms act to construct women as 'Other' so that women are only what men are not' (Woodward, 1997: 36–37), understood as different, deviant or a threat.

The resources that accrue to the One in the binary divide are rarely the subject of scrutiny. As discussed above, while women are often viewed as *disadvantaged* in occupying the lower levels of the occupational structure, the organization and pay scales in general, the factors that support the *relative advantage* of men go unnoticed. As such, the privileges that accompany masculinity go unremarked – hidden within the norm.

Unmasking the privilege and resources of masculinity

Since the 1990s, the notion that men are 'gender free' has been increasingly disrupted. Displaced from its common-sense status as an unnamed, universal moral referent, white masculinity as a category of gender identity has been appropriated by both critical and non-critical commentators (Giroux, 1997). Critical studies of gender in general and masculinity in particular view gender difference as a social construction rather than as a natural biological category with a view to denaturalizing the idea of masculinity as the privileged place of gender normativity. The primary aim of these critical accounts '. . . is to unveil the rhetorical, political, cultural and social mechanisms through which (masculinity) is both invented and used to mask its power and privilege' (Giroux, 1997: 382).

Connected to this and as part of a strategy of identity politics, marginalized groups such as women have involved themselves in political practices and mobilizations constructed around social and cultural identities (Robinson, 2000; Kusz, 2001). These activities involve the marking of women as victims of discriminatory practices both currently and in the past. As Kusz points out:

> Within the logic of identity politics minority subjects (women, people of colour, and gays and lesbians) took the offensive by arguing that their oppressed and marginalized positions were a direct result of the privileged positions of the dominant groups . . . . . One notable change within these backlash offensives of the 1990s was that . . . White masculinity was increasingly marked publicly as the oppressive invisible centre. (2001: 396)

Occupancy of the norm is therefore never secure and, as the above suggests, can be the site of struggle as other groups such as women seek to 'unseat' the privileged from the dominant centre. Groups which desire more recognition accordingly position themselves against the norm by claiming disadvantage and thereby promoting the visibility of social difference. The privileges that attend the centre are thus rendered more visible and men, hitherto 'unmarked' as a gender and universalized within the norm, become marked as a particular (racial) and gendered group. As Robinson suggests, while white men have resisted the process of 'marking', they have been partly 'de-centred' (removed from their occupancy of the norm) and this has helped to increase the visibility of both gender and race.

Backlash: the male victim and the quest for visibility

While these struggles helped to expose and make visible the normative and invisible character of masculinity, a backlash emerged which contested the representation of men and the masculine as oppressive, dominating, uncaring and socially and economically privileged. Men (in particular white men) as a group started to engage in identity politics of their own, constructing themselves as victims of contemporary change. According to Robinson (2000: 3) 'invisibility is a privilege enjoyed by social groups . . . . . but it can also be felt as a burden in a culture that appears to organize itself around the visibility of differences'.

In this sense it can be argued that men are now taking on an active gender identity. No longer can we simply understand men as the invisible, disembodied mentality of the human while women are embodied in their biological sex (Mills, 2003). Men (particularly white men) are being visibly reconfigured to the world as victims as a means of counteracting the critical attempt to make men visible as an advantaged elite, whose privilege derives from their dominance of disadvantaged groups.

In this respect, over the past decade continuous concern has been voiced about a perceived crisis that men are facing connected to unemployment, changing family patterns, failure in school and violent crime. According to Beynon (2002), the summer of 2000 could justifiably be described as the 'masculinity-in-crisis-summer'. The contemporary crisis faced by men is believed to be particularly evident in work organizations where men face constant job role changes, the threat of redundancy, job-related stress and an increasingly competitive labour market with men in middle management positions experiencing growing levels of alienation (Beynon, 2002). Despite their continued dominance of the corporate world, it is suggested that men are now subject to unprecedented challenges, obstacles and disadvantage.

The identification of this 'disadvantage' lies along side suggestions that prospects have never been better for women (Oakley, 2000). Women's 'advantage' is believed to manifest itself in a number of ways from job advertisements which state that applications from women and other minority groups are particularly welcomed to instances where men appear to be explicitly excluded from positions in organizations. A recent example of such exclusion occurred during a recruitment campaign run by the Avon and Somerset Police, which along with other police forces in the United Kingdom are seeking to ensure that the profile of their workforce adequately reflects the population that they are policing. In a bid to achieve this aim, Avon and Somerset Police rejected 200 applicants to the force because they were white and male (*The Times*, 2005). It is suggested that such incidents contribute to a sense of male disadvantage leading to what some commentators have referred to as male backlash against the personal consequences for men that may attach to the pursuit of equality (Mobley, 1992; Heilman, 1994; Burke & Black, 1997).

Backlash emerges when historically advantaged groups such as men blame another group (e.g. women) for problems such as fewer promotion prospects or job opportunities. The phenomenon of male backlash is conventionally associated with men's exclusion from equality programmes leading to material disadvantage. Though men can avail of the protections provided by equality legislation and equality policies, as a group they are not the original 'target' of such initiatives because of their historically (and continuing) advantaged position. In this sense men exist 'outside' of the contemporary equality regime, constructing themselves as victims of as opposed to participants in, the campaign for equality for women and other minority groups.

From this perspective men orchestrate a backlash against their 'marginalization' claiming that they are suffering from a type of reverse discrimination where women and other minority groups are benefiting at their expense, though such 'discrimination' is almost impossible to determine. For example, the American Equal Employment Opportunity Commission found that out of 3000 discrimination opinions in the federal courts between 1990 and 1994, only 100 cases concerned reverse discrimination with the charge being upheld in only six of these. Nevertheless, despite this material reality, as Anderson (2005) suggests, the perception of reverse discrimination has been planted in the minds of many.

Backlash and competing victim syndrome

In the literature on male backlash a differentiation is made between two types of men based on their orientation to the principle of equality. First, there are those who initially agreed with equality but whose support has declined due to the perceived harm they claim they experience as concrete steps are taken to bring equality about. Second, there are men who have always opposed equality, believing instead in the 'rightness' of traditional roles for women. This opposition is increasingly displayed as the pursuit of equality appears to threaten their position.

While some commentators (e.g. Goode, 1982) reserve the term backlash for the first category of men, others such as Burke and Black (1997) and Leck (2002) believe that it applies to both groups. According to Mobley (1992), male backlash is intensified by a number of factors including a lack of communication within an organization about equality and diversity initiatives; the exclusion of men from the development of equality programmes; the blaming of men for the disadvantage experienced by minority groups such as women; the refusal to perceive men as part of the solution to inequality as opposed to its cause. Research indicates that backlash can be more intense in those organizations that have the greatest success in recruiting non-traditional employees (Mobley, 1992; Gilbert & Ivancevich, 1999). What these accounts of the phenomenon of backlash have in common is their positioning of men as observers outside of the equality project, being affected (negatively) by it but not influencing it in any positive sense (Robinson, 2000).

Commentators such as Cox (1996: 221) have referred to backlash as a 'competing victim syndrome', where it is claimed that men are subject to similar injustices and oppressions as those experienced by women and that feminism has overstated male privilege. Though male backlash is a recurring historical phenomenon, emerging during those historical junctures where women appear to be achieving some form of equality, backlash is believed to be stronger now (Faludi, 1991). The strength of contemporary manifestations of backlash derives from the juxtaposition of what is seen as women's disproportionate 'advantage' derived from the new equity regime, alongside men's perceived 'disadvantage' connected to organizational restructuring and economic change. Rather than understanding this situation as the consequence of two separate but overlapping processes, it is suggested that backlash occurs because it is easier for men to direct resentment and antagonism at women who appear to be doing well, as opposed to an organizational environment and economy that is beyond their control (Leck, 2002).

Backlash and the struggle over normativity

The targeting of women as the cause of masculine economic decline, contributes to a masking of the negative impact of industrial restructuring and a highly individualist competitive economic order, on traditional male occupations. The notion of backlash also operates to conceal men's continued economic advantage (higher pay, more opportunities, occupation of senior positions.) over women and other disadvantaged groups. Even if male economic resource is under pressure, it is still superior to that of women (Kusz, 2001) and herein lies the crux of male backlash.

While on the surface the notion of backlash may appear to be a regrettable though 'understandable' response to competitive tensions around access to economic resources, it is also important to recognize that the deeper struggle over how we conceptualize our world, how we define what is the norm, takes place through backlash politics. In other words male backlash is not only a 'singular pitched battle' between men and women centred on access to material resource, it is fundamentally a '…complicated struggle over normativity…' which is '…constantly under revision (and) shifts in response to the changing social, political and cultural terrain' (Robinson, 2000: 4). In this sense the phenomenon of backlash is both a material and a symbolic struggle. As Robinson argues, men are involved in a conflict over cultural priority and their construction of themselves as victims is not simply to demonstrate how they 'suffer' materially from the pursuit of equality, but rather acts to curtail the power of equality discourses to transform the dominant discourse that supports masculine power.

Ideologies of work and representations of the normative worker are always shaped and expressed in relation to material circumstances. In other words, how we think about the world of work and the schemas we develop in understanding work are deeply articulated with material resources (Lewis, 2004a). The closer that individuals or groups represent the normative, the easier it is for them to secure access to and control of those resources. However the power to represent the normative can never be taken for granted and must be constantly re-won – and in this respect, as Robinson (2000) argues, the battle for the ability to define and represent the terms of the normative is being fought through backlash politics. Accordingly, men and masculinity have a vested interest in being *both visible and invisible*, with *victim visibility* acting as a means of maintaining *victor invisibility*. Through the backlash struggle men seek to maintain the advantages of invisibility while seeking to be made visible as a victim – rather than as a victor who has managed to keep a firm grip on the materiality of his privileged status.

Visible victims, invisible advantage

This is not simply opportunism on the part of men or a cynical manipulation of the cultural power which attaches to the identity of 'victim'. Rather the ever changing distinctions between being on the inside or outside, being included or excluded '. . . exercises a pull that even the most privileged seem unable or unwilling to resist' (Robinson, 2000: 8). Such claims of victimization normally require individuals giving up their claim to individuality and taking on a collective identity, for example, member of the discriminated group 'men'. Though this has the potential to be a troubling experience for historically privileged individuals (Robinson, 2000), it can act as a significant challenge to critical attempts to highlight the privilege attached to male invisibility. While critical scholars have sought to render men visible as dominant oppressors, the representation of men as *victims* acts as a means of disavowing and denying the structural privileges of masculinity that have been highlighted and critiqued by critical writers over the past two decades (Kusz, 2001).

From this perspective the take-up of the status of victim is an attempt by men to construct a visible gender identity which is characterized by *disadvantage* and not advantage. The construction of historically privileged groups as disadvantaged, acts as a mechanism to secure and maintain privileged normativity along with access to material advantage, while simultaneously denying the existence of such advantage. The contemporary argument that men are now in a precarious and vulnerable position, largely due to the implementation of equality initiatives over the past three decades seeks to do two things. First it allows men to be visible on their terms and counter charges of invisible advantage and second it acts to maintain the dominant cultural and material position of men (Kusz, 2001). In other words, claims of victimization and the construction of a visible and collective gender identity based on supposed inequality serves to cloak and hence conceal and deny continuing structural privileges of masculinity under the mantle of claimed disadvantage.

The female victim and the quest for invisibility

While men seek to achieve the visible status of victim, women are involved in a quest of their own. Over the past three decades the identity politics that women have been involved in have provided significant possibilities for empowerment. Women have established a presence in occupational positions within both public and private organizations from which historically they have been formally and legally excluded. Nevertheless, despite the formal equality which women now supposedly possess, the notion of the universal 'individual' as discussed above, does not encompass everyone. Diverse bodies considered as belonging to 'Other' places are deemed to be 'out of place'.

In this sense, women despite their increased presence are defined as and experience themselves as 'space invaders' (Puwar, 2004). As 'space invaders' it is argued that women have to pay considerable attention to the management of their gender, adhering to the social rules of femininity while at the same time making sure they are not too feminine. According to Puwar (2004: 75) an '. . . excess of femininity could result in them being labelled as hysterical. Located in an organization based on a masculine performance, a fine balanced fusion of femininity and masculinity has to be enacted'.

However, more and more women lack or refuse to accept a self-conscious understanding of themselves as gendered actors, eschewing the notion of managing their femininity. Instead women are framing their response to work situations within a gender-neutral account of organizations (Smithson & Stokoe, 2005; Lewis, 2006). Studies of women (e.g. Rhodes, 1988; Piderit & Ashford, 2003) in senior organizational and professional positions suggest that they often treat the suggestion of gendered organizations and gendered experiences as 'taboo' in recognition of the substantial professional risk that attaches to it. However issues of gender are not just seen as 'out of bounds' within work contexts, increasingly this position is reinforced by the contemporary belief that the problem of gender disadvantage has been 'solved' (this idea was discussed within the context of women's voice literature in Chapter 2).

In this respect, journalistic accounts of the 'gender question' speak of the end of patriarchy and the gender order and of a significant increase in women's opportunities (Oakley, 2000; Whitehead, 2001b). This assertion of a gender-neutral social context is reinforced by women's commitment to the notion of merit, discussed in Chapter 2, contributing to the emergence of a gender-blind ideology which claims that gender is no longer important. Women's silence on gender issues and their adherence to a gender-blind ideology might be the price they are willing to pay to gain access to main-stream executive culture (Olsson, 2000).

Alternatively, acceptance of this ideology might be more than the pragmatic paying of a price for career success. Rather women also appear to be actively trying to become invisible, avoiding being marked and symbolically con-structed as 'the Other' (Lewis, 2006). By maintaining a silence on gender, in particular the masculinist paradigm in which management and organizations are embedded, and by understanding their experience of work as the ability to abide by 'universal' standards of professional work behaviour, women are trying to avoid being identified as different from the masculine norm. In other words, rather than seeking to de-centre men from their normative position, some women seek assimilation into the norm.

Men as Other and struggles around the dominant centre: the case of male nurses

Some men identified as Other (e.g. by their occupational choice), may also seek assimilation into the norm. This is evidenced by struggles and tensions as male nurses seek inclusion into the 'dominant centre' of their organizations, colonized by white male doctors. Unlike women, who in a recent study of male nurses were presented as being far removed from the 'dominant centre' or norm ('too deferential', 'too unassertive' or lacking specialist knowledge and expertise), men minimized differences between themselves and male doctors as members of that 'elite' group. This was affected through attitudes and practices which drew on ties of fraternity and on the common status of (rational) masculinity.

> I do have a close relationship with the (male) doctors – I find that I can be pally with them and sit down and chat with them and we can talk about men things

However, entry was never complete or fully secure and there was frequently tension around male nurses' uncertain status in relation to this 'norm'. Tension was evidenced in stories of encounters with (always male) doctors where norms of deference and of hierarchy were challenged and overturned.

> I've sent doctors out of my unit before – I've sent them off because I felt they were behaving inappropriately in front of my patients and I've said don't come back to my unit until you either apologize or you can conduct yourself appropriately

In this respect, the position within the norm, the location of the One, can become the focus of struggle, tension and resistance. This can lead to divisions and alliances which concern the processes and experiences of marking and difference. Men in nursing, marked through their association with the feminine and where women represent the unmarked case, draw on ties of fratriarchy to seek assimilation into the dominant centre. Visible as gendered subjects in their occupational contexts (e.g. through common references to 'male' nurses rather than nurses per se), this can be seen as an attempt to gain some of the attendant privileges of invisibility and status associated with the norm. Therefore, while work on conflicts around the norm has tended to assume that it is minority groups (such as women) who fight to *de-centre* white men as the symbol of 'universal personhood' this suggests that individuals can instead seek to attain invisibility and *assimilation* into the norm. However, men express the tensions associated with their contradictory position as both One (as men) and Other (as male nurses) by subverting the norms of deference associated with the privileged status. Responses to marking and the associated subjectivity of Other can accordingly be seen in aggressive displays whereby men attempt to challenge the dominant position.

Extract from Simpson (2006): Men in the Margins: Visibility and Difference when the One Becomes the Other and is Positioned Outside the Norm, paper presented at the ASCOS conference, Auckland.

While as the above example suggests, some groups of men can lie outside the dominant centre (or norm) and be marked as 'men', a key question to consider here is how easy or difficult is it for women, as a systematically disadvantaged group, to adopt a gender-free guise. How can women take on the mantle of invisibility and connect into the privilege of assimilation into the norm which has historically benefited men? Is it possible for women to 'tap into' or reverse the institutionally embedded white masculine advantage and the silent representation of the white male body as the 'universal' body (Puwar, 2004)?

The difficulties are substantial. Just as the white male body is taken to be the norm in most work situations, particularly professional and leadership positions, the female body is associated with activities such as nurturance and care located mainly, but not exclusively, in the private realm. For example, as Smithson and Stokoe (2005) argue with reference to childcare issues and work-life balance, the use of the 'generic she' or 'generic female parent' implicitly assumes that the mother and not the father is responsible for childcare. Thus even where women may eschew a gendered subjectivity, the assumed gendered subjectivity of all women, which has at its centre the importance of caring responsibilities, will affect them. Though individuals might choose not to enact a 'gender display', presenting themselves as much as possible in a gender neutral way, they cannot prevent others from seeing them and treating them as either gendered male or female (Lewis, 2006).

In this sense, both men and women are members of the series 'men' and the series 'women' (Young, 1994). Referring to men and women as belonging to a series allows us to distinguish between an active, felt, internalized identity and the material conditions and social reality in which a person is located. The seriality of gender means that though men and women do not necessarily take up gender as an active identity, it still essentially moulds individual lives (Lewis, 2004a). Men and women (whether they like it or not) are part of and shaped by a gender existence. For men membership of the series 'men' translates into a direct advantage where their way of being in the world is taken as the norm, as the standard by which all others must abide. For women membership of the series 'women' can act as a disadvantage by accentuating their difference from the norm, hindering their attempts to conceal their gender as a means of securing the invisible cloak of normality and universality.

Conclusion

In this chapter we have explored deep conceptualizations of invisibility. In particular the chapter has sought to demonstrate how men in highly gendered societies have an invisible gendered identity which bestows on them considerable economic and social advantage. While we are well used to accounts of work experiences which seek to demonstrate how the gendered identity of 'woman' is a burden for women seeking to participate in the workforce in the same way as men do, we are less used to accounts of gender which demonstrate how maleness functions as a direct advantage.

This advantage derives from the positioning of the universal body as a white male body, '.. one that is beyond bodily particularity, while the others remain marked by their gender or racial positioning' (Puwar, 2004). Recent critical studies have sought to reinsert men into history as a means of exposing their privileged position and questioning individualistic and decontextualized notions of success and failure. Though men may not take up an active gender identity, gender still fundamentally shapes their lives through better access to scarce resources and through the absence of the economic and social disadvantages experienced by women (Lewis, 2004a). In looking at deep conceptualizations of invisibility the chapter has drawn on research which has sought to break the silence surrounding the masculine self so that it cannot remain as an unchallenged norm.

In addition the chapter has also considered the response to such critical challenges. In particular it has explored the notion of male backlash, focusing on the representational strategy of defining men as victims of the contemporary pursuit of equality. Focusing on the issue of why men want to be perceived as 'victims' as opposed to whether there is empirical support for men's claims of victimhood, the chapter has considered how the phenomenon of backlash is more than a dispute over access to material resource – it is also a symbolic struggle over normativity.

Finally this chapter briefly considered an emerging contemporary response to women's continued economic disadvantage. Instead of emphasizing the inequalities women still experience, some women are themselves struggling for the status of invisibility and the associated privilege of assimilation into the norm. Thus for both men and women there is advantage attached to being both visible and invisible at one and the same time.

6

Exploring masculinity studies through voice and visibility

Introduction

As the previous chapter points out, men and masculinity have been both visible and invisible in academic theorizing and research. Their supremacy in accounts of organizational behaviour, exemplars of managers, entrepreneurs and workers, renders them visible against the invisibility of women. At the same time, their universal status and alignment with the norm means they are seen as people rather than men and as such are 'opaque to analysis' (Hearn, 1994). Men are therefore everywhere in studies of work and yet are invisible as gendered subjects. As Morgan (1992) argues, the terms work, working and men are nearly always interlinked so that the disembodied worker is seen as male – without work-family conflict and favouring a traditionally masculine demeanour. Masculinity is therefore a basic but implicit feature of the organizational ideal type.

Men and masculinity have consequently only recently been the subject of critique or interrogation. Rather than accepting power relations as located within stable structures or within individuals, this approach focuses on the dynamic nature of power and how it is dispersed within social practices and social relations. In the United Kingdom, what became known as Critical Studies of Men was pioneered by Hearn (1985, 1987) who sought to dismantle men's assertions to universality and to explore masculinity as dynamic patterns of ideologies and practices constructed and negotiated in interaction. Therefore, the critical study of men and masculinity is oriented towards seeing gender as dynamic, shifting and often contradictory and has taken the focus off women as the (one and only) gendered subject and a 'problem' to be explained.

In this chapter, we challenge the traditional view in organization studies that treats men as generically human and which associates gender with women's problems and issues and explore how we can apply the concepts of voice and visibility at a 'surface' and at a 'deep' level to an understanding of masculinity and work. We start with an overview of the development of masculinity studies and then locate the different perspectives within our surface and deep conceptualizations. This location has been made on the basis that each of the four main perspectives within masculinity studies presented in this chapter (role theory, the social relations perspective, psycho-analytic accounts and post-structuralism) can be associated with one particular aspect of surface or deep visibility or voice. We also evaluate the different perspectives in terms of the extent to which they can be seen to incorporate these levels of analysis. In so doing, we go some way to 'bring masculinity in' to a more generalized gender framework.

The meaning of masculinity

A good starting point is to consider what we mean by masculinity. Several possibilities have been proposed, for example, 'what it means to be a man' (Kimmel, 1994); a configuration of practice within a set of gender relations (Connell, 2000); 'those behaviours, languages and practices which are commonly associated with males and thus culturally defined as not feminine' (Whitehead & Barrett, 2004).

The range of definitions is evidence of the 'slipperiness' of the concept. However, what they share is an agreement that masculinity is relational in that it does not exist in isolation but with reference to its opposite, namely femininity – and furthermore that masculinities and male behaviour go beyond simple genetic predispositions to encompass cultural and social components. As such, as Collinson and Hearn (1994) point out, far from being foundational on biology, masculinity represents discourses and practices that indicate someone is a man. In fact, as Sedgwick (1985) has argued, masculinity cannot always be equated with men and, rather than seeing masculinity and femininity as a dichotomy, it may be more useful to conceptualize them as different perpendicular dimensions such that some people may score highly on both. While it may be difficult to come up with a single definition of masculinity, it is possible to agree that masculinity does not refer to individual possessions – but to institutionalized practices located in structures of power.

The development of masculinity studies

Prior to the development of masculinity studies in the 1980s men had been the focus of scholarship but in an uncritical, a-gendered and unproblematic way. As we have seen in Chapter 2, different theories have attempted to break the dominance of men's accounts of social life and have highlighted the *absence and neglect* of women's voices and experiences. Not surprisingly, they put aside further considerations of men and masculinity beyond an acknowledgement of their role, through patriarchy, in women's oppression (had they not heard enough about men already?). Masculinity was therefore 'left aside' – a unitary notion within patriarchy which attained universal status as a single cause of women's oppression (Mac An Ghaill, 1994). Male behaviour and masculine attitudes and values were subsumed under this single concept which, as some feminists writing on women (e.g. Acker, 1989, 1990; Walby, 1990) as well as some feminists writing on men (Hearn, 1994; Connell, 1995, 2000) have argued, denies agency, complexity and contingency through its monolithic, a-historical, biologically over-determined status.

As a single, overarching factor, patriarchy therefore oversimplifies the structure of gender. Instead, gender relations are multi-dimensional and differentially experienced within specific organizational contexts. As Connell (1987) has argued, patriarchy is accordingly likely to be interwoven in complex ways with features of the organization such as hierarchy, managerial control, resistance and inequality. As such, Connell (1987) developed concepts such as hegemonic masculinity, the culturally exalted form of masculinity which guarantees the dominant position of men, to highlight the multidimensional and socially constructed aspects of male dominance, the precarious nature of masculine identities and men's contradictory experience of power (Connell, 1987; Hearn, 1987; Segal, 1990; Collinson, 1992; Kaufman, 1994). These issues are explored in more detail below.

Masculinity studies and related work on gendered power therefore grew out of a recognition of the limitations of the concept of patriarchy in explaining men's experiences and the implications of their attitudes and behaviours. Some frameworks accordingly emerged to analyse and document the material, social and discursive production of masculinity.

Frameworks within masculinity studies

As discussed above, frameworks within masculinity studies have largely rejected the monolithic status of patriarchy, which underpins early feminist literature as the single cause of women's oppression and have focused on ways in which masculinity is constructed, its multidimensionality as well as how it is experienced in different contexts. Four dominant frameworks have emerged from the literature (Carrigan et al., 1985): role theory, the 'social relations' perspective, psychoanalytic approaches and post-structuralist accounts.

We align these perspectives within surface conceptualizations of voice (role theory) and visibility (the social relations perspectives) and within deep conceptualizations of voice (post-structuralism) and visibility (psycho-analytic perspectives). This alignment has been made on the grounds that in each case there are certain overlaps suggesting that one particular aspect of our conceptualization can be applied to a theoretical orientation more readily than others.

The role perspective and surface conceptualizations of voice

Role theory, which has some associations with our surface conceptualization of voice in that both support traditional notions of gender difference, developed in the 1950s and 1960s to examine the changing role of men in the post-war period – particularly in relation to the erosion of traditionally 'masculine' jobs, the rise in divorce rates and the encroachment of women into hitherto male preserves in the public arena. Role theory conceptualized sex roles as acquired or learned through socialization. Behaviour of men and women as well as their respective social positions are explained through reference to conformity to norms and by appealing to the social expectations that defines proper behaviour for women and for men. All social behaviour is therefore learned, or 'internalized', through socializing 'agents' (e.g. school, family, media). Society is thus organized around a differentiation between men and women's roles and this can be seen to be of benefit to society in the form of stability and order (e.g. Parsons, 1951).

Role theory suggests that men conform to norms and expectations regarding appropriate 'male' behaviour. As such, it underpins and provides an explanation for gender difference as outlined within the women's voice perspective discussed in Chapter 2. Men (and of course women) accordingly learn specific ways of leading and of managing so as to conform to expectations of gender roles. In terms of leadership, role theory would suggest that men manage 'transactionally' (Rosener, 1990), that is, through direction and control, because they are conforming to gender roles. Equally, with reference to work on gender differences in communication styles (e.g. Cameron, 1998), men dominate conversations by interrupting and challenging others because they have been socialized to do so. The overbearing nature of male voices, in management and other arenas, can thus be seen as the result of socialization processes and conformity to norms.

Both orientations (role theory, surface conceptualizations of voice) support and reinforce a binary view of gender based on differences between men and women. Both see gender and hence masculinity as fixed and unchanging, with an orientation towards *static* difference and on stable factors that are seen to constitute that difference in the form of learned and/or biologically determined roles. Role theory therefore shares much of the underlying assumptions of surface conceptualizations of voice, which as we saw in Chapter 2, is based upon *states of difference* between men and women.

However, rather than attempting to highlight the voices of a particular group such as those of women (as in the women's voice perspective), role theory gives equal weight to men's and women's experiences in that they are both seen as the result of socialization. Unequal outcomes, through the dominance of men, are justified and naturalized through conformity to norms and the functions thus performed for a harmonious society. Masculinity, as a set of power relations, is thus invisible – evading scrutiny or problematization behind a cloak of essential difference. Furthermore, gender from this perspective is seen as something connected to women but not men. While men are visible as a (stable) category, they are invisible as a gender. While their voices predominate, they are not recognized as 'din' (Harlow et al., 1995), that is, as the noise which dominates and silences others. Overall, the absence of any theory of male power in role theory led to subsequent work on the dynamics of masculinity and the dialectical processes and practices of gender relations (Connell, 1987; Hearn, 1987; Kaufman, 1987; Kimmel, 1994) – thus laying the foundations for more critical work.

The social relations perspective and surface visibility

Role theory gives an abstract account of supposed differences between men and women rather than an analysis of the relations between them – so playing down the power that men exercise over women. The 'social relations' perspective (Carrigan et al., 1985) examines how gender makes up and is reflected in structures of power relations and the ways in which social practices are organized as sets of social relations. On this basis, masculinity is viewed as a set of *distinct practices* (e.g. Tolson, 1977; Connell, 1987) which take shape in particular institutions such as the class system or at work. This has some association with our surface conceptualization of visibility in that both focus on gender through the relations between men and between men and women (e.g. relations of dominance and subordination) and on gender as a set of practices (e.g. practices of marginalization and of role trap enforcement).

Tolson (1977), for example, focuses on the significance of class and father-son relationships, influenced particularly by the father's position in the labour market, for constructions of masculinity. While masculinity is associated with the world of work and with power, working class men have little power. They are therefore more likely than middle class men to dominate at home and to adopt a macho identity to counterbalance the powerlessness in their jobs. For middle class men, the construction of masculinity is characterized by 'psychic hardening' within a competitive hierarchy epitomized in the public schools as well as in many work contexts. Capitalism therefore draws men into a network of social relations that encourage sets of behaviours which we would recognize as typically male.

Similarly, Connell (1987) explores structures of social relations and how the patterning of these relations makes up a 'gender regime' within an institution. Power relations incorporate patriarchy, that is, the subordination of women and domination of men; production relations refer to the gendered division of labour and its effects in the form of higher male wages and male control of capital accumulation and enterprise; emotional relations capture male dominance in heterosexual partnerships and in sexual relations while, in his later work (Connell, 2000) symbolism refers to gendered processes of communication through, for example, language, dress and body culture. These relations and associated practices help make up the 'gender regime', that is, the patterning of these relationships within an institution. The underlying principle therefore is that gender is a social practice and masculinity is a configuration of that practice.

The social relations perspective can be aligned with some foundational aspects of 'surface' visibility and masculinity, discussed in Chapter 4. Both focus on practices of behaviour and gender relations in specific organizational contexts. Drawing on Kanter's work on the largely detrimental effects of visibility for token women (in the form of marginalization, exclusion from informal networks and forced conformity to stereotypical roles), research has suggested that heightened visibility can be associated with specific practices and relations that are advantageous to men. For example, as we have seen, men working in non-traditional occupations have been found to benefit from visibility through assumptions of enhanced leadership and by being associated with a more careerist attitude to work (Floge & Merril, 1986; Heikes, 1992;

Simpson, 2004, 2005). A set of practices based on traditional notions of gender therefore arise which serve to support men and fast track their careers – from being encouraged to attend management courses to being given challenging and development opportunities at work.

At the same time, men adopt specific material practices which seek to distance them from the feminine associations of the job – choosing more masculine specialisms in nursing (such as mental health or accident and emergency), taking responsibility for sport in teaching and attempting to identify and align themselves with the (masculine) dominant centre of organizations (doctors, consultants, head teachers). Through these practices, men support a masculine identity and separate themselves from the mundane and 'feminine' roles of service and care. Unlike Kanter's work, which assumes the negative effects of high visibility for women will be eroded with increased numbers, such work recognizes the advantages of visibility for men through the positive cultural valuation given to masculinity. As Connell, arguing from a social relations perspective, suggests patriarchal relations at work and a gendered division of labour give rise to practices that afford men an advantage and help to secure a position at the top.

The social relations perspective therefore sees masculinity as a social construction, institutionalized in structures and practices as well as in face-to-face relationships. These relations and practices will vary from one institution to another – and may co-exist with other forms across and even within institutional contexts. Different masculinities may exist within an organization such as a hospital or a school where a masculinity organized around professionalism and care may coincide with an equally compelling masculinity at managerial levels based on hierarchy and control.

Work on surface conceptualizations of visibility as applied to men and men's experiences in organizations explores the nature of gender relations in the context of male tokenism and the material consequences in the form of gendered practices when men 'stand out in the crowd'. As such, it conforms largely to the parameters of the social relations perspective through its emphasis on gendered practices as well as on the nature of social relations in different institutional contexts.

Unlike the social role perspective, this more critical approach makes men visible as the dominant gender and goes some way to help understand the source of that dominance beyond the simple learning of a role. However, it does not locate men or masculinity within the invisibility of the norm or draw systematically on the concept of discourse to understand the dynamics of gender relations. These deep conceptualizations can be understood more fully through the psycho-analytical and post-structuralist frameworks to which we now turn.

Psychoanalytical approaches

Psychoanalytical accounts focus on the psychic investments that individuals have in dominant sexual and gendered discourse, with masculinity historically defined as a flight from and repudiation of the feminine (e.g. Chodorow, 1978; Hollway, 1994; Kimmel, 1994). Men and masculinity are located within the norm with women and femininity devalued as Other. In this respect, this perspective can be aligned with deep conceptualizations of visibility discussed in the last chapter – where the dominant centre is largely invisible to analysis.

Drawing on Freud's Oedipal complex which charts boys' attempts to replace their deep emotional attachment to the mother with identification with the father, work within psychoanalytical approaches has focused on the precarious construction of male identity through the renunciation of the feminine as well as the accompanying fear of being seen as less than masculine (a 'sissy') by other men. In Freudian terms, the male child learns to devalue all women to demonstrate to the father the accomplishment of manhood. Fears concerning the negative judgements of men as well as an associated flight from the feminine are therefore driving forces behind constructions of masculinity.

While rejecting the masculinist assumptions within Freudian theory (i.e. a tendency to justify and naturalize male domination), other work has drawn on this framework to analyse gender relations. Chodorow (1978), for example, sees men as having a fear of 'regressing' to the feminine and to the state of unity with the mother. They therefore develop a need to differentiate from women and denigrate the feminine in themselves. Similarly, Kimmel (1994) uses the concepts of homosocial enactment (the constant scrutiny of other men) and homophobia (fear of homosexuality) to examine masculine behaviour.

Homosocial enactment, as Kimmel argues, comes about because ideologies of manhood have functioned primarily under the gaze of male peers and male authority (women have such a low place on the social ladder that female judgement is of no consequence!). Homophobia, or fear of homosexuality, occurs because early identification with the mother means the boy sees the father through her eyes, that is, as an object of sexual desire. During later identification with the father, that sexual desire must be suppressed. One result is a fear of intimacy with other men as well as a need to control emotions that are associated with the (rejected) Other of femininity. This can be seen, according to Kerfoot and Knights (1993, 1998) in masculine attitudes and endeavours such as an instrumental rationality towards career and the lonely pursuit of power and control at work.

If masculinity involves the rejection of femininity and homosexuality, then women and gay men become the 'Other' against which heterosexual men project their identities. The concept of the Other contains the opposition to self. As Hollway (1994) argues, women are Othered through the Oedipus complex as separation from women and the denigration of femininity occurs. Establishing boundaries between self and the Other, to separate, distinguish and validate that self, is a continual struggle and source of anxiety as men project unwelcome parts of themselves (e.g. the vulnerable, the emotional, the weak) onto others of different and often inferiorized categories. In this way they experience themselves as living up to a masculine ideal. In the context of the gendered division of labour in organizations, for example, conceptualizations of 'men's work' relies on the Other of women's work in order to invest it with a masculine status.

This orientation to Other has specific relevance for deep conceptualizations of visibility. This locates men, as invisible and hence powerful, within the norm and those outside the norm as Other. As part of the 'dominant centre' (Hearn, 1996), men see themselves and are seen by others as the taken for granted, universal standard case. Their bodies are 'unmarked' in the sense that they are not defined by their category (men) and so carry no detrimental social significance. As 'invisible gendered subjects' (Whitehead, 2001b), they evade damaging essentialization and scrutiny. Inhabiting an unmarked body (disembodied from gender, disembodied from sexuality or procreation) is thus to be privileged and to be 'immune from focused critique' (Hearn, 1994: 614). As Robinson (2000) argues, invisibility is a necessary condition for the perpetuation of male dominance – masculinity escapes surveillance and regulation because it is hidden from view.

In order to secure a position within the norm (as the One), the dominant must differentiate themselves against a lesser Other. In this respect, women are 'marked', that is, categorically defined as women, and made to embody gender while men remain unmarked and invisible within the norm. Women, as Other, are therefore the visible reference point for gender issues and as such represent or are the embodiment of gender problems. As we saw in the last chapter, the dominant, by contrast, have an interest in remaining unmarked and invisible – in itself a source of power. It is those in the margins, the Other, who have an interest in promoting the visibility of social difference, for example, by highlighting male privilege and gender inequalities. This renders men visible as a category and partly de-centres them from their dominant position.

Deep conceptualizations of visibility, by drawing on the concept of the Other as well as locating men and masculinity within that norm, therefore has some associations with psycho-analytic frameworks. As Mac An Ghaill (1994) argues, psychoanalytical theories may account for how masculine identities get reproduced through patterns of relations which define women as Other (to be repudiated and spurned), but the power of men over women is assumed rather than explained. Moreover, as (Whitehead, 2001b) points out, the framework is ultimately in tension with a notion of masculinity as variable and fluid as well as a dynamic of power relations and may serve to reinforce rather than disrupt the binary divide. So while men are rendered visible as gendered subjects in these accounts, they say little about the factors that lie behind the dominance (the din) of men's voices and the sources of male power – and, as in the social relations perspective, do not take on board the dimensions and diversity of masculine identities. In this respect, they overlook the power of discourses, as in deep conceptualizations of voice, in the construction and maintenance of male power.

Post-structuralist explanations and deep conceptualizations of voice

Role theory sees masculinity as a largely stable and static category grounded in biology or acquired through socialization; within the social relations perspective, men's identity is dependent on institutions and constructed through a set of social relations which exist over and above the individual action of men while psycho-analytical approaches are oriented towards an inner (and unchanging) masculine self aligned closely with psycho-sexual development. None of these approaches can fully account for the dynamics of gender or the significance of agency in power relations. More recently, work on masculinity has focused on the role of agency and how masculinity is experienced at a subjective level as well as on the influences of institutions and social practice. This 'post-structuralist' perspective (Connell, 2000) explores the dynamic nature of masculinity, how it is constructed and reconstructed, how it is experienced at a subjective level and how multiple masculinities exist in relation to the dominant (hegemonic) form. We equate this perspective with deep conceptualizations of voice through its focus on the power relations inherent in discourse and through the significance afforded to the ability of dominant discourses to silence competing meanings.

As we discussed in Chapter 3, post-structuralists draw on the concept of discourse, that is, signs, labels, expressions and rhetoric to explore how meaning is constructed and maintained. Discourses serve to shape our thinking, attitudes and behaviour as well as our sense of self. Language, both written and spoken, is open to multiple interpretations and, through inclusion and exclusion, can privilege some meanings and interpretations over others. We hear some voices and are deaf to others because the meanings dominant voices convey are privileged and powerful and sit comfortably with our assumptions and ways of seeing the world. Other meanings, which may challenge these attitudes and values, are accordingly silenced. In this way language and practice interact.

In so far as gender is also a meaning that is produced through discourse, post-structuralists seek to explore how masculinity and femininity are defined in local situations and how these definitions influence organizational behaviour as well as our identity. In short, post-structuralists see masculinity (and of course femininity), not as the products of biology, child development or socialization, but as *discursively* produced. A deep conceptualization of voice therefore captures the power of discourse as well as the process of silencing that occurs as dominant meanings and interpretations are conveyed.

Multiple discourses, multiple masculinities

The above suggests that masculinity does not exist prior to social interaction but comes into existence as people act and communicate in local situations. Masculine identities are consequently produced through interaction – always in process and never fully accomplished. If there is no 'core' self and if identity is in this way a product of discourse, then there will be a multiplicity of identities dependent on local institutions and interactions. Therefore, by moving away from seeing gender as a stable category of the individual (as in role theory and psycho-analytical interpretations), and by placing emphasis on its dynamic and contingent nature, post-structuralists open up the possibility to multiple masculinities in any context. Boyle (2002), for example, revealed four different types of masculinity in a study of the male-dominated para-medical services: militarized masculinities (characterized by inflexibility, rigidity and hierarchy associated with a military past), managerial and techno masculinities (characterized by bureaucratic control and a growing technological, as opposed to emotional, focus), heroic masculinities (reflecting the deferential and admiring attitudes from members of the public) and nurturing masculinities (reflecting the caring and emotional demands of the job).

Dominant discourse and hegemonic masculinity

As Connell (1995) argues, at any one time and in any context there will be a dominant or 'hegemonic' masculinity. Hegemony refers to the cultural dynamics by which a group claims and sustains a leading position. Hegemonic masculinity is the culturally exalted form – an idealized version– which serves to stabilize and underpin the gender order and to legitimize patriarchy. This particular type of masculinity – the most honoured or desired – is hegemonic because it has imposed a particular definition of 'what it means to be man' on other kinds of masculinity, which are marginalized or subordinated as a result. Hegemonic masculinity can be expressed and represented in everyday inter-actions as well as through other representations such as the media and the state. Connell (2000) suggests that hegemonic masculinity has the following features:

1. It is at the centre of the system of gendered power and serves to legitimize gendered relations of domination and subordination.
2. It is based on the subordination and marginalization of women.
3. It is emphatically heterosexual, thus homophobia and fear of being thought homosexual is an important mechanism of hegemony in gender relations.
4. It equates manhood with toughness – being strong, successful, capable, reliable and in control.

These dominant discourses are evident in a variety of situations. They are acted out in sport and can be seen in the machismo of many popular Hollywood films – as well as in the corporate displays of masculinity at top levels of business, the military or government. As we saw in Chapter 3, dominant discourses maintain their hegemonic status by drawing on and reinforcing other generally accepted meanings. In this respect, we saw how the values and practices associated with masculinity and management under-pin and support each other – and so contribute towards the dominance and 'din' of male voices and of male interests at work. We also saw that to maintain their hegemonic status, dominant discourses must be able to silence or dis-credit alternative ways of seeing the world. Hegemonic masculinity therefore shares a set of meanings that are oppositional to common assumptions around femininity – as well as homosexuality – and depends on their sub-ordination or exclusion.

In this way, masculinities can be seen to exist as discourses – dominant and subordinated ways of thinking, talking and acting and the means by which males 'become' men (Whitehead & Barrett, 2004). In constant movement with each other, some masculinities are hegemonic in the sense that they are perceived to be the most desired form. However, hegemonic masculinity is not a fixed character type – always and everywhere the same. As Connell (2000) points out, this 'type' occupies the hegemonic position in a given pattern of gender relations and, while it is likely to embody most of the features above, it is a position that is always contestable. For example, recent images of the footballer David Beckham cuddling his baby and of Tiger Woods crying on winning a golf championship are symbolic of a new amalgamation of traditional masculinity based around sporting prowess and a masculinity that is concerned with nurturing, care and emotions, culturally associated with femininity and previously rejected from the traditional hegemonic ideal.

While, as we saw in Chapter 3, privileged voices and dominant discourses maintain their dominant position by silencing other voices as unsuitable or excessive, such silence is rarely complete – if only because the very process of 'naming and shaming' gives those voices and orientations an existence and so possibility of future authority. Therefore, while suppression and rejection of the feminine has been part of maintaining hegemonic masculinity, there are instances where attributes culturally associated with femininity have been successfully incorporated into a new masculine ideal.

Discourse, contradictions and insecurity

Post-structuralists accordingly draw on the significance of meanings and interpretations (i.e. discourse) and of local understandings for the construction and negotiation of identities. On this basis, given that the individual experiences multiple discourses within his or her social field (Kerfoot & Knights, 1993), identity can be seen as contingent, fluid and fragmentary. Moreover, given the likelihood of discourses cross-cutting or sitting in an uneasy relationship with one another and of some discourses displacing others, identity will additionally be ambiguous, insecure and uncertain (Kerfoot & Knights, 1998; Collinson, 2003) – leading to internal conflict and contradiction.

This tendency towards contradictions and insecurity may well be exacerbated for men as they position themselves against the hegemonic ideal. As Connell points out, the culturally exalted 'blueprint' of masculinity while evident in some contexts, such as the army or in sport, may only correspond to a small number of men (how often do men get the opportunity to display 'rugged masculinity'?). There is thus a tension between this collective ideal and the reality of men's lives. Positioned, as is often the case, 'unfavourably' against this model, masculine identities must be negotiated, defended, achieved in every day situations. Men therefore strive to prove the unprovable – that they are fully 'male'. Exacerbated by the erosion of rigid gender definitions from the challenges and gains of women, manhood is therefore chronically insecure and a source of pain and alienation (Kaufman, 1994). As Kaufman suggests, the effects can be seen in the rise over the last two decades of 'week-end warriors' – groups of men who attempt to return to 'essential manhood' through a variety of outdoor exploits.

Similarly, as Kerfoot and Knights (1998) argue in the context of work, a precarious masculinity can be underpinned by management and hierarchy. Hierarchical structures organized around power and authority, can give a sense of security to men for whom insecurity about their identity (in relation to this unattainable ideal) leads to a need to control. In this way, a stable sense of self is sought through the compulsive pursuit of 'ever escalating goals and achievements' often founded on core managerial assumptions that plans, objectives and techniques can render the future controllable (Hearn, 1994). By fixing identities within stable structures of formally ascribed relations of superiority and subordination, hierarchies can therefore provide the ideal conditions for holders of positions of managerial authority for the pursuit of secure masculine identities, otherwise threatened by a perceived failure to reach the supreme hegemonic goal.

Overall, we have established that at the 'deep' analytical level of voice, masculinity can be seen as a product of discourse. Masculinity take many different forms with some 'voices' dominating and marginalizing others. These masculinities sit in some relationship to the dominant hegemonic form, which comprises a largely unattainable blueprint for the majority of men. As a result, masculine identities are insecure and precarious and often call upon other related discourses and practices such as management and hierarchies, to support its cause. At the same time, masculinity strives to marginalize, ridicule or suppress competing discourses (e.g. around femininity) in order to help shore up pretensions to the hegemonic ideal. This post-structuralist perspective can be equated, as argued earlier, with deep conceptualizations of voice through the shared focus on discourse as a source of gender power and through the role of silence in the maintenance and reproduction of that power.

This post-structuralist perspective therefore takes as its starting point the dynamics of gendered power and how the 'din' of male voices silence and marginalize others. At the same time, it recognizes the power of silence in suppressing and eliminating alternative experiences and views. This 'deep' conceptualization can add to our understanding of the noise of male voices (surface) in particular contexts. For example, the voices of men in the board-room or in ordinary conversations are underpinned by the dominance of masculine discourses. We hear these voices and they carry weight and noise (surface) because they emanate from privileged frames of meaning and because they draw on rhetoric, naming and language as well as on silences which sustain that privilege (deep). It is male voices that often draw on rhetoric around conquest, competition, targets, control as well as adjectives that denigrate women. The ability of men to control conversations and to interrupt women (surface) is therefore partly predicated upon the dominance of masculinist discourses (deep) in many organizational and broader societal contexts.

Conclusion

Taken together, frameworks within masculinity studies have attempted to redress the monolithic status of patriarchy, seen by many (in particular radical) feminists as the single cause of women's oppression and so reducing the complexity of gendered power relations to a single cause. In their different ways, the frameworks paint a more complex picture of male behaviour and development of masculine attitudes and values. This is done through a focus on socialization into gender roles, the patterning of relations within particular gender regimes, psycho-sexual development and the associated rejection of the feminine 'Other' and the way masculine identities are discursively produced and acted out in specific contexts. In this chapter, these perspectives have been associated with (although by no means exclusive to) surface conceptualizations of voice (role theory) and visibility (social relations perspective) and similarly with deep conceptualizations of voice (post-structuralists) and visibility (psycho-analytical accounts). This is summarized in Figure 6.1.

The location of these masculinity perspectives within our framework has been made on the basis that they can be applied to one particular aspect more readily than others. The associations are therefore not to be seen as 'set in stone' to the extent that some overlaps and blurring of boundaries occur. Psycho-analytic accounts have some resonance with role theory in that the former seeks to explore the underpinnings of self when respective roles are adopted; role theory may merge into the social relations perspective as the adoption of roles 'spills over' into practices and influences gender relations; post-structuralists, as well as those from the psycho-analytical framework, draw on the concept of Other in their analysis of the production of identity. These overlaps inevitably have implications for the associations with the surface and deep conceptualizations of voice and visibility presented in this chapter.

We have also drawn these conceptualizations to evaluate the different perspectives within masculinity studies. Thus, in role theory men are visible as a stable category but invisible as a source of gendered power; male voices are seen as dominant but not recognized as 'din' in their power to silence others. The location of men and masculinity within an invisible norm and the power of discourse in gender relations go unrecognized. Within the social relations

Social role perspective

Socialization and conformity to gender roles as the source of male behaviour

Supports traditional notions of gender as states of difference between men and women

Men invisible as a gender

Men's voices dominate (through socialization and role conformity) but overlooks power of discourse to silence other voices

Associations with surface accounts of voice

Post-structuralist perspective

Gender as discursively produced and masculinity as discourse

Focus on the dynamics of gender, and the fluid, unstable and insecure nature of masculine identities.

The power of masculine discourses to silence competing meanings

Masculinity is visible as a source of power relations

Associations with deep accounts of voice

Social relations perspective

Gender as a practice and a stable set of (patriarchal) relations as seen through gendered divisions of labour and the advantages of visibility for men in token positions

Men more visible as the dominant gender

Men's voices dominate (through patriarchal relations and practices) but overlooks power of discourse to silence other voices

Associations with surface accounts of visibility

Psycho-analytical perspective

Masculinity as repudiation of the feminine

Women as gendered 'Other'

Men's fear of the male gaze

Men and masculinity as invisible within the norm

Men invisible as a gendered group

Associations with deep accounts of visibility

Figure 6.1   Masculinity studies through the concepts of voice and visibility.

perspective, men are rendered visible as a gender and we can go beyond socialization processes to appreciate the 'din' of male voices in silencing others – but the power of discourse remains underdeveloped and there is little recognition of the power struggles that occur around the norm. Recent psycho-analytical approaches locate men and masculinity, as the One within the norm, and women as Other but take little account of the power of discourse to frame gender meanings while post-structuralists go beyond surface conceptualizations to systematically explore the role of discourse and of silence in maintaining and reproducing gendered power.

These commonalities and overlaps notwithstanding, surface and deep conceptualizations of voice and visibility help to highlight key aspects of the different perspectives, the ways in which they relate to each other and, at the same time, to recognize those aspects which in some orientations remain silent or hidden from view.

7

Overview and an application of the framework to female entrepreneurship

Introduction

In this book, we have explored gender and organizations through the twin concepts of 'voice' and 'visibility'. In gender studies, as in other areas, the concepts have been used at different levels of abstraction to analyse inequality and exclusion. However, we have argued that their potential richness has not been fully exploited and we have accordingly adopted a framework of analysis which is based on 'surface' and 'deep' conceptualizations, presented and discussed below. With 'voice', we therefore distinguish between the 'surface' act of speaking/being heard as discussed within 'women's voice' literature (Chapter 2) and, at a deeper level, the power of silence as discursive practices eliminate certain issues from arenas of speech and sound (Chapter 3). Similarly, we can see visibility as a 'surface' state of exclusion and difference associated with numerical disadvantage (Chapter 4), while at a deeper level, conceptualizations can usefully explore the power of 'invisibility' and the battle for the (male) norm (Chapter 5). While recognizing the influence of radical feminism in some women's voice research, we have located these levels within liberal feminist and post-structuralist interpretations, respectively.

In this final chapter, we summarize and explain the framework that has been developed in the book. We then 'operationalize' the framework by applying it to the literature of gender and entrepreneurship. Finally, we examine connections across and between the levels of analysis and consider some inherent contradictions and paradoxes. In so doing, we discuss how these tensions help us to further our understanding of some of the dynamics inherent in the gendering of organizations.

Overview of the framework of deep and surface conceptualizations of voice and visibility

As we saw in Chapter Two, a surface level literature on voice has focused mainly on women's experiences in order to redress their 'weak presence' in theory and practices of organizations and the emphasis is on giving voice to women's knowledge and understandings. In so doing we have acknowledged the strong influence of this perceptive on the uptake of solution and resolution discourses as women make sense of their lives. Research has focused on exploring *differences between* men and women. Drawing on Chapter Four, the literature of visibility at this conceptual level has been oriented towards an analysis of the structures of organizations and the significance of numerical balance for 'token's experiences at work. Inequality is accordingly viewed as a state of exclusion and difference where visibility is associated with *difference from* the majority group. Both are informed by liberal feminism – assuming gender to be an unproblematic category of the individual and seeing organizations as gender neutral, stable structures – though, as we discussed in Chapter One, there are radical feminist influences in the valorization of the feminine in some pro-women's voice leadership research (Figure 7.1).

At a deep conceptual level, and with reference to Chapter 3, work on discourse provides a means of exploring the processes whereby some voices are privileged over others and how some dominant discourses (e.g. around masculinity) silence and suppress other discourses (e.g. femininity) in order to maintain their dominant position. In other words, deep conceptualizations of voice seek to demonstrate how discourse constructs and defines difference – rather than charting *states* of difference between men and women or *states* of difference from a numerically dominant group. The more limited work on invisibility, outlined in Chapter 5, also goes beyond surface states of inequality to explore the invisibility of the norm and the processes by which men maintain power through their occupancy of the normative position. While women's voice literature emerged to redress the 'weak presence' of women, deep conceptualizations of (in)visibility and the norm are predicated upon the strong (though invisible) presence of men. This presence is a source of struggle as other groups (e.g. women) seek to de-centre men from their privileged position or seek invisibility through attempts to assimilate into the norm. Deep conceptualizations of voice and visibility are strongly influenced by post-structuralist interpretations which see power as dispersed within discursive practices and which place emphasis on the dynamic nature of gender and struggles around the norm.

	Voice	Visibility
Surface conceptualization	Inequality seen as a state of absence and neglect (weak presence)	Inequality seen as a state of exclusion and difference
	Emphasis on giving voice to difference and to women's experiences	Visibility seen as a numerically disadvantageous state
	e.g. women in management literature	Focus on material practices and implications for women as 'tokens'
	pro-women's voice transformational leadership research	Invisibility associated with the power of the majority
	Draws on liberal and radical feminist principles	Draws on liberal feminist principles
Deep conceptualization	Processes of silencing through discourse	Processes of maintaining power through invisibility of the norm (strong presence)
	Focus on the power of silence and silence as an agent of power	Contestations over the normative state and demands for visibility
	Focus on masculinity as hegemonic discourse	Focus on white masculinity as disembodied normativity
	Broadly post-structuralist interpretation	Broadly post-structuralist interpretation

Figure 7.1   Surface and deep conceptualisations of voice and visibility.

Applying the framework: gender and entrepreneurship

To further illustrate how the framework can be applied as an organizing principle, we now consider the literature around gender and entrepreneurship. Such work, as discussed by Simpson and Lewis (2005), has reflected to a large extent the development of ideas outlined above while at the same time has raised issues around the silencing of gender and femininity within discourses of entrepreneurialism and around the transparency of the (male) entrepreneurial norm.

Surface conceptualizations of entrepreneurship through voice and visibility

At a surface level, and from the perspective of women's voice literature, work over the last two decades has moved away from an unproblematic focus on male entrepreneurs as the universal case to the inclusion of women's accounts and experiences (Carter, 2000; Carter & Weeks, 2002). Such research has tended to concentrate on the motivations to set up business and specific challenges women face. In line with the liberal feminist emphasis on 'gender justice', prescriptions have been sought to remove or reduce the negative impact of (female) gender (e.g. by ensuring fair and equal access to capital and finance). Most studies, as with the majority of women's voice literature, were built around comparisons with men (e.g. Marlow, 1997) and resulted largely in different typologies of the female entrepreneur (e.g. Goffee & Scase, 1983, 1985). In common with this literature, and its focus on 'surface states' of absence and neglect, such work gives voice to women's experiences as a valid and neglected area of work.

Other works have explored issues of visibility associated with 'token' status and the material consequences of exclusion from the dominant group. In as much as female entrepreneurs currently make up only 26 per cent of the self-employed population in the United Kingdom (Carter, 2000), this group can be seen to carry the burdens of visibility. In this respect, Carter (2000) has highlighted the consequences of the exclusion of female entrepreneurs from formal and informal networking and Lewis (2004b) has discussed some of the disadvantages (such as lack of credibility) associated with the domestically orientated mother/wife 'role trap' of the female entrepreneur. One consequence of negative stereotyping and the high visibility associated with minority status, is the experience of 'performance pressure' (Kanter, 1977) and the need for women to prove themselves as 'serious entrepreneurs' in the eyes of men (Lewis, 2006). Therefore, in common with 'surface' conceptualizations discussed previously, such work can be interpreted in terms of the consequences of visibility associated with the pressures of 'difference' and of their exclusion or marginalization from the dominant group.

Deep conceptualizations of gender and entrepreneurship through voice and visibility

Both these 'surface' conceptualizations of female entrepreneurship share the same limitations outlined earlier in relation to liberal feminism. Both conceive of gender as stable categories which adhere to the individual and assume gender-neutral organizational contexts. Conforming to our 'deep' conceptualization of voice and silence, a growing literature has contested the notion that gender can be conceived of as an addition to neutral entrepreneurial processes, viewing it instead as a vital part of those processes. A major focus of such work concerns the importance of discourse for constructing our understandings of gender and of entrepreneurialism as well as for the subjectivity of the 'entrepreneur' (e.g. Carr, 2000; Bruni et al., 2004). Such understandings draw on rhetoric of enterprise (discovery, exploration, commitment, risk) as well as on symbolic meanings around heroism, initiative, leadership and self-reliance and point to their location within the masculine domain. Kerfoot and Knights (1998), for example, make links between the rhetoric and associated discourses of entrepreneurialism and competitive masculinity, arguing that these sustain and reproduce a variety of (controlling, instrumental, goal-oriented) masculine behavioural displays.

As we have seen, in order to maintain their privileged positions, dominant discourses must silence and devalue competing meanings and interpretations (e.g. Calas & Smircich, 1999; Gabriel et al., 2000; Wray-Bliss, 2002). The dominant discourse of enterprise and entrepreneurialism, currently privileged in many areas of organizational life (du Gay, 1996), can therefore be seen to be constructed on a valorization of 'masculine' vales and attributes as outlined above. These are embodied in conventional ('male') entrepreneurship models which emphasize size, growth and profit (Lee-Gosselin & Grise, 1990; Fenwick, 2002) while alternative ('female') ways of organizing based, for example, around stability and work-life balance are devalued and silenced, through negative labelling and rhetoric of 'non-serious' business (Lewis, 2004b). As Calas and Smircich (1999) argue, by delineating and setting limits on what is 'said', silences and absences help to confer legitimacy on the meanings conveyed. Accordingly, our 'knowledge' of the entrepreneur as embodying qualities of pro-activity, commitment and risk, culturally associated with masculinity, is predicated upon the silences around 'female' meanings of passivity, adaptability and a desire for security. In this way, a hierarchical arrangement between said and unsaid is established and the 'ontological priority' (du Gay, 1996) of hegemonic (masculine) entrepreneurship is maintained.

As Bruni et al. (2004) and Lewis (2006) argue, the gender as variable approach has rendered invisible the masculinity inherent in these (entrepreneurial) activities. As we have seen, in being judged against a normative standard, the difference of minority individuals is made visible and highlighted while the norm itself, by reason of its transparency, evades scrutiny and essentialization. Accordingly, the behaviour of women involved in entrepreneurial activity is defined and evaluated against the standards of an invisible masculine norm which, as Carr (2000) suggests, encompass the conventional 'masculine' model of a dynamic profit-oriented growth business. This has contributed to the 'othering' of the non-male, so that women are 'marked' (as *female* entrepreneurs rather than as entrepreneurs per se)

	Voice	**Visibility**
Surface conceptualization	Highlights absence and neglect of women from accounts of enterprise	Highlights the token status of female entrepreneurs
	Seeks to include women's voices and experiences (e.g. through typologies of female entrepreneurs)	Focus on role traps (e.g. of mother/wife)
	Focus on gender justice and equal opportunities	Highlights pressure of difference from the majority group
Deep conceptualization	Importance of discourse in constructing meanings around enterprise	Focus on the invisibility of the masculine norm in enterprise which universalizes the male model
	Focus on enterprise as a privileged (and masculine) discourse	Women Othered and marked/ categorized by their gender
	Processes of silencing of alternative meanings of enterprise	

Figure 7.2   Viewing gender and entrepreneurship through the framework of voice and visibility.

and categorized as 'non-serious' business (Lewis, 2006). By making masculinity invisible, the male entrepreneurial model is accordingly universalized and stripped of gender.

This analysis is summarized in Figure 7.2.

Surface accounts of gender and entrepreneurialism therefore adopts a 'gender as variable approach', highlighting the role of stereotypes and the pressures and barriers they face in comparisons with men. Deep conceptualizations by contrast places gender, as a social process in enterprise, at the heart of the analysis. Drawing on 'deep' conceptualizations of voice, the significance of silence in discourse and of the power relations inherent in the relationship between the said and unsaid can be recognized and can contribute to our understanding of the 'doing' of gender in diverse contexts such as enterprise. Equally, drawing on 'deep' conceptualizations of visibility, the transparency of the male entrepreneurial norm can be problematized and a recognition of the 'Othering' of the non-male and of alternative ways of organizing can help to uncover what has been hitherto been concealed.

The framework thus acts as a useful heuristic in 'mapping' specific literatures within the field of GOS while at the same time alerting us to possible gaps in interpretation. Thus we can move on from the simple inclusion of women's voices to consider the significance of absence and silence in specific discursive regimes; we can understand the behaviours of women in some contexts as a quest for invisibility while, as discussed previously, a status of visibility can in other arenas be sought by some men. The explanatory potential of the framework – of surface and deep conceptualizations of voice and visibility – is considered in more detail below.

Connections *across* the levels

While we have examined 'surface' and 'deep' voice and visibility as separate conceptualizations, as in the above application, with different theoretical orientations and underlying assumptions and values, we suggest that it is possibly in combining the two that a greater understanding can be achieved. First, some connections exist *across* both surface and deep conceptualizations (i.e. looking at horizontal comparisons on the framework).

At a surface level, both visibility and voice relate to states of inequality associated with absence and neglect (voice) and with exclusion and difference (visibility) with little regard for underlying processes. The focus is largely on women and women's experiences and there are close, but not exclusive, associations with liberal feminism. However, while women's voice literature has a specific focus on giving voice to difference and to acknowledging women's experiences, literature on visibility is more concerned with the material practices and implications for women as members of a numerically minority group. The former therefore is concerned with the individual while the latter has organizational structures at the centre of analysis.

By the same token, at the deeper conceptual level, there are overlaps between the power of silence within discourse (the unsaid) and the power of invisibility associated with the norm (the unseen). Both involve processes of domination and suppression and place power relations at the centre of analysis. Here the focus is on masculine attitudes and behaviour and on processes of retrenchment and resistance that take place as existing gender power relations are simultaneously underpinned and challenged. Deep conceptualizations of voice allows us to understand how the din of male voices silence and suppress those of women, while deep conceptualizations of visibility captures the 'crisis of masculinity' experience as a response to de-centring from the norm. In fact, drawing on both conceptualizations of voice and (in)visibility at this level, Chapter 5 highlighted how the din of male voices is being challenged by women and other historically disadvantaged groups through discourses of equality and multiculturalism. This has led to a de-centring of men from the norm and a possible backlash and crisis in (white) masculinity.

Connections *between* the levels

At the same time, there are close associations *between* the two levels of abstraction (i.e. looking at vertical comparisons on the framework).

Looking at voice, to appreciate why women's voices have been neglected or gone unheard (surface) we need to understand the power of dominant discourses in conveying appropriate meanings, and of the role of silence in dominant discursive regimes (deep). In this respect, masculine experiences and interpretations are given priority and appear as universal (masculinity as a hegemonic discourse). At the same time, men command a language to convey these meanings while a similar language to express the experience of oppression can escape women as a marginalized group (there is, for example, a wide and colourful range of words that can be used to denigrate women – bitch, slag, cow – while there are few words for women to draw on to similarly express their anger against men).

Similarly, with visibility, in order to understand the material practices associated with numerical imbalance, we need to acknowledge the power of (in)visibility and the significance of its location to the norm – as well as the conflict and resistance that occurs around the normative state.

In other words, the problems women encounter through the heightened visibility of a token status in organizations (surface) can be understood more fully by locating men and masculinity as invisible within the norm (deep). Outside the norm, women are 'marked' as a devalued, deficient Other – an embodiment of difference – and accordingly marginalized from the majority group.

Tensions and paradox

The above suggests that the framework can also highlight certain tensions and paradox. For example, analytical principles within the framework may help to resolve the tension between academic theorizing, which places emphasis on the centrality of gender in understanding organizational behaviour, and the voices of women who argue that organizational practices and processes are gender free. We have seen that women are often reluctant to acknowledge gender as an issue and accordingly deny the salience of gender in their organizational lives (e.g. Rhode, 1988; Piderit & Ashford, 2003; Lewis, 2006). The voices of women would therefore suggest a diminishing or eradication of gender disadvantage in contemporary contexts. However, the effort that some women make to 'keep gender out' demonstrates their unacknowledged awareness of its centrality to assessments of their performance (Lewis, 2006). An examination of the 'unexpressed' and of silence can therefore yield insights that are different from or go beyond the 'surface' meanings conveyed in voices and text.

'Deep' conceptualizations of (in)visibility may also highlight other divisions and alliances which relate to the process of marking and struggles around the norm. These groupings are likely to be concealed by focusing solely on *differences between* male and female as exemplified within women's voice literature or *difference from* the majority group as in 'surface' conceptualizations of visibility. Accordingly, as we have seen from Lewis's study discussed above, in aligning themselves with the world of men, female entrepreneurs were in conflict with counterparts who, in their eyes, conformed to the 'feminine' stereotype and so did not aspire to the male model of 'serious' enterprise. As such, they were seen to damage the reputation and credibility of all entrepreneurial women. Therefore, by refusing to accept the existence of difference between male and female entrepreneurs and by understanding their experience of entrepreneurship as the ability to abide by 'universal' (male) standards of good business, some women hoped to evade 'marking' by creating distance from any practices or values which were thought to exclude or marginalize them.

While work on the battle for the norm has tended to assume that it is minority groups who fight to de-centre white men as the symbol of 'universal personhood' (e.g. Robinson, 2000), this suggests that conflict can occur *within* the minority group as individuals struggle for the status of invisibility and the privilege of assimilation into the norm. Accordingly, conflict can occur between men around the dominant centre of organizations – as evidenced by the level of antagonism displayed by male nurses (as Other) to male doctors (the One) where male doctors are more securely located within that privileged space.

Furthermore, we can see that it is possible to have a vested interest in being both visible and invisible. On one level, we saw in Chapter 5 that *victim visibility* is a means of maintaining *victor invisibility*. Men seek through the backlash struggle to be visible as victims and so keep the material advantages of masculinity hidden from view. Men therefore benefit from visibility (as victim) and invisibility (of their material advantage).

At another level, both visibility and invisibility can be seen to have positive links with power. Invisibility has an alliance with power for some groups through their occupancy of the normative position. Members are consequently 'unmarked' and so fail to attract surveillance and discipline. At the same time, visibility can be associated with power and influence for those who are struggling for recognition and who previously have been hidden from view. Power is therefore associated both with the invisibility of the norm and with visibility for those demanding change. This paradox can be partly explained by the differential location of (in)visibility to the norm. On this basis, the power of invisibility lies in its incorporation with the norm. Outside the norm, however, to be invisible is to lack power so that heightened visibility is required to gain recognition and to challenge the normative state. By positioning (in)visibility in relation to the norm, this 'deep' conceptualization incorporates an analysis of power with processes that keep certain dominant groups hidden and beyond scrutiny.

Theoretical tensions and overlaps

In discussing surface and deep conceptualizations of voice and visibility, we have drawn on different theoretical perspectives. These have pertained to liberal and radical feminism (surface explanations) and post-structuralism (deep explanations). In this respect, previous work has tended to treat perspectives on gender as analytically and conceptually distinct (e.g. Savage & Witz, 1992; Halford et al., 1997; Halford & Leonard, 2001). However, there may be potential in exploring overlaps and interconnections as well as contradictions between them.

Surface conceptualizations of both voice and visibility have roots in liberal feminism with women in management literature sharing with liberal feminism a notion of equal right to scarce resources and 'gender justice' (Calas & Smircich, 1996). However, as we saw in Chapter 1, while early liberal feminism sought to claim equal status and *similarity* with men (based on an unproblematic male norm), later work, influenced by the radical feminist valorization of the feminine over the masculine (e.g. Ferguson, 1984), focused on ways in which women were *different* from men. One key impact of radical feminism therefore has been through the central place that is now given to difference (Hatcher, 2003) in considerations of gender. This influence has contributed to the emphasis by some women's voice literature on female difference as an asset (e.g. the value placed by Rosener on the female-oriented 'transformational' leadership style) and has gone some way to challenge the male norm as the benchmark for gender comparisons. As such, radical feminism may be positioned as 'enlightened correction to liberal inspired research' (Calas & Smirich, 1996: 231). The place of radical feminism in GOS is accordingly secure, not because it is extensively used as a perspective in and of its own right, but rather because of the considerable influence its emphasis on difference has had on liberal as well as post-structural feminism.

In fact, as Calas and Smirich (1992) argue, while women's voice literature stands in 'tension' to post-structural feminism in that the former gives a (largely radical feminist) priority to women's voices while the latter problematizes the privileging of any voice, this perspective is a necessary step for making post-structural feminism viable. This is because the women's voice perspective reveals the absence of women's values in organizations and a body of work (e.g. Gilligan, 1982; Rosener, 1990) 'inverts' oppositional constructions of male and female by prioritizing the female. This paves the way for post-structuralists to explore how symbolism around 'woman' creates boundaries to discourse and helps to maintain the 'normality' of hierarchical structures as well as to question the possibility of sustaining claims to any privileged voice or experience. Therefore, while separate consideration of surface and deep conceptualizations has some value in contributing to our body of knowledge on gender and organizations, it is in combining the two that more powerful inferences can be made (Simpson and Lewis, 2005).

Summary

This book has reviewed gender and organization literature through the twin concepts of voice and visibility. In so doing, we have helped to provide a level of coherence to the diverse ways in which the concepts have been used and have thereby gone some way to strengthen their potential as analytical principles. By drawing attention to 'surface' and 'deep' conceptualizations, located broadly but not exclusively within liberal feminist and post-structuralist perspectives, and by highlighting the complexities of the relationships within and between them, we have contributed to an understanding of the gendering of organizations and the theoretical development of the field. Through our framework, we have uncovered the complex ways in which the concepts have been used, their relationship to each other and have drawn attention to potential contradictions, overlaps and connections. As we have argued elsewhere (Simpson and Lewis, 2005), while the creation of a framework presupposes boundaries and divisions (between deep and surface, between voice and visibility), separate analysis is a necessary precondition for subsequent exploration of tensions and interdependencies. In other words, in order to fully exploit the potential of the different conceptualizations of voice and visibility, we need first to understand their conceptual power as separate categorizations before exploring ways in which they support and contradict one another. As argued earlier in this book, it is through exploring such interdependencies and tensions that we can develop a richer understanding of gender processes in organizations.

References

Acker, J. (1989) 'Making Gender Visible', in R. A. Wallace (Ed.) *Feminism and Sociological Theory*. Newbury Park, CA: Sage.

Acker, J. (1990) 'Hierarchies, Jobs, Bodies: A Theory of Gendered Organizations', *Gender and Society*, 4 (2): 139–158.

Alimo-Metcalfe, B. (1994) 'Gender Bias in the Selection and Assessment of Women in Management', in M. Davidson and R. Burke (Eds) *Women in Management: Current Research Issues*. London: Paul Chapman Publishing, pp. 93–109.

Alvesson, M. (1998). 'Gender Relations and Identity at Work: A Case Study of Masculnities and Femininities in an Advertising Agency', *Human Relations*, 51 (8): 969–1005.

Alvesson, M. & Due Billing, Y. (1992) 'Gender and Organization: Towards a Differentiated Understanding', *Organization Studies*, 13 (12): 73–102.

Alvesson, M. & Due Billing, Y. (1997) *Understanding Gender and Organizations*. London: Sage.

Alvesson M. & Karreman, D. (2000) 'Varieties of Discourse: On the Study of Organizations through Discourse Analysis', *Human Relations*, 53 (9): 1125–1149.

Anderson, T. H. (2005) 'The Strange Career of Affirmative Action', *South Central Review*, 22 (2): 110–129.

Ashcraft, K. L. & Mumby, D. K. (2004) *Reworking Gender: A Feminist Communicology of Organization*. Thousand Oaks: Sage.

Bagilhole, B. (2002) *Women in Non Traditional Occupations: Challenging Men*. New York: Palgrave Macmillan.

Belenky, M., Clinchy, B., Goldberger, N. & Tarule, J. (1997) *Women's Ways of Knowing: The Development of Self, Voice and Mind*. New York: Basic Books.

Beynon, J. (2002) *Masculinities and Culture*. Buckingham: Open University Press.

Blau, P. (1970) 'A Formal Theory of Differentiation in Organizations', *Administrative Science Quarterly*, 27: 35–65.

Blau, P. (1977) *Inequality and Heterogeneity*. New York: Free Press.

Bologh, R. (1990) *Love or Greatness: Max Weber and Masculine Thinking – A Feminist Enquiry*. London: Unwin Hyman.

Bowen, F. & Blackmon, K. (2003) 'Spirals of Silence: The Dynamic Effects of Diversity on Organizational Voice', *Journal of Management Studies*, 40 (6): 1393–1417.

Boyle, M. V. (2002) 'Sailing Twixt Scylla and Charybdis: Negotiating Multiple Organisational Masculinities', *Women in Management Review*, 17 (3/4): 131–141.

Bradley, H. (1993) 'Across the Great Divide', in C. Williams (Ed.) *Doing Women's Work: Men in Non-Traditional Occupations*. London: Sage.

Bruni, A., Gherardi, S. & Poggio, B. (2004) 'Doing Gender, Doing Entrepreneurship: An Ethnographic Account of Intertwined Practices', *Gender, Work and Organization*, 11 (4): 406–429.

Burke, R. J. & Black, S. (1997) 'Save the Males: Backlash in Organizations', *Journal of Business Ethics*, 16 (9): 933–942.

Burke, R. & McKeen, C. (1994) 'Career Development Among Managerial and Professional Women', in M. Davidson and R. Burke (Eds) *Women in Management: Current Research Issues*. London: Chapman.

Burke, R., Rothstein, M. & Bristor, J. (1995) 'Interpersonal Networks of Managerial and Professional Women and Men: Descriptive Characeristics', *Women in Management Review*, 10 (1): 13–25.

Butler, J. (1990) *Gender Trouble: Feminism and the Subversion of Identity*. New York: Routledge.

Butler, J. (1993) *Bodies that Matter*. London: Routledge.

Butler, J. (1999) *Gender Trouble: Feminism and the Subversion of Identity*. London: Routledge.

Butterfield, D. A. & Grinnel, J. P. (1999) 'Reviewing Gender, Leadership and Managerial Behaviour: Do Three Decades of Research Tell Us Anything?', in G. N. Powell (Ed.) *Handbook of Gender and Work*. Thousand Oaks, CA: Sage.

Byrne, D. (1971) *The Attraction Paradigm*. New York: Academic Press.

Calas, M. & Smircich, L. (1991) 'Voicing Seduction to Silence Leadership', *Organization Studies*, 12 (4): 567–602.

Calas, M. & Smircich, L. (1992) 'Using the F word: Feminist Theories and the Social Consequences of Organizational Research', in A. Mills and P. Tancred (Eds) *Gendering Organizational Analysis*. Newbury Park, CA: Sage.

Calas, M. & Smircich, L. (1996) 'From the Woman's Point of View: Feminist Approaches to Organization Studies', in S. Clegg, C. Hardy and W. Nord (Eds) *Handbook of Organization Studies*. London: Sage.

Calas, M. & Smircich, L. (1999) 'Past Post-modernism: Reflections and Tentative Directions', *Academy of Management Review*, 24 (4): 649–671.

Cameron, D. (1995) *Verbal Hygiene*. London: Routledge.

Cameron, D. (1998) 'Performing Gender Identity: Young Men's Talk and the Construction of Heterosexual Masculinity', in J. Coates (Ed.) *Language and Gender*. Oxford: Blackwell, pp. 270–284.

Carr, P. (2000) *The Age of Enterprise*: *The Emergence and Evolution of Entrepreneurial Management*. Dublin: Blackhall Press.

Carrigan, T., Connell, R. & Lee, J. (1985) 'Towards a New Sociology of Masculinity', *Theory and Society*, 14 (5): 551–604.

Carter, S. (2000) 'Gender and Enterprise', in S. Carter and D. Jones-Evans (Eds) *Enterprise and Small Business: Principles, Practice and Policy*. Harlow: Pearson Education.

Carter, S. & Weeks, J. (2002) 'Introduction to Special Issue on Gender and Business Ownership: International Perspectives on Theory and Practice', *The International Journal of Entrepreneurship and Innovation*, 3 (2): 81–82.

Chartered Institute of Personnel and Development (2005) *Training and Development: Annual Survey Report*. London: CIPD.

Chodorow, N. (1978) *The Reproduction of Mothering*. Berkeley, CA: University of California Press.

Clegg, S. (1989) *Frameworks of Power*. London: Sage.

Cliff, J., Langton, C. & Aldrich, H. (2005) 'Walking the Talk? Gendered Rhetoric vs Action in Small Firms', *Organization Studies*, 26 (1): 63–91.

Coates, D. (1998) 'Gossip Revisited: Language in All Female Groups', in J. Coates (Ed.) *Language and Gender*. Oxford: Blackwell, pp. 226–253.

Cockburn, C. (1985) *Machinery of Dominance: Women, Men and Technical Know-How*. London: Pluto Press.

Cockburn, C. (1991) *In the Way of Women: Men's Resistance to Sex Equality in Organizations*. London: Macmillan.

Coe. T. (1992) *The Key to the Men's Club*. Corby: Institute of Management.

Collinson, D. (1992) *Managing the Shopfloor: Subjectivity, Masculinity and Workplace Culture*. Berlin: Walter de Gruyter.

Collinson, D. (2003) 'Identities and Insecurities: Selves at Work', *Organization*, 10 (3): 527–547.

Collinson, M. & Collinson, D. (1996) 'It's only Dick: The Sexual Harassment of Women Managers in Insurance Sales', *Work, Employment and Society*, 10 (1): 29–56.

Collinson, D. & Hearn, J. (1994) 'Naming Men as Men: Implications for Work, Organization and Management', *Gender, Work and Organization*, 1 (1): 2–22.

Collinson, D. & Hearn, J. (1996) '"Men" at "Work": Multiple Masculinities/Multiple Workplaces', in M. Mac an Ghaill (Ed.) *Understanding Masculinities: Social Relations and Cultural Arenas*. Buckingham: Open University Press.

Connell, R. (1987) *Gender and Power*. Cambridge: Polity Press.

Connell, R. (1995) *Masculinities*. California: University of California Press.

Connell, R. (2000) *The Men and the Boys*. Cambridge: Polity Press.

Coward, R. (1999) 'Women are the New Men', *The Guardian*, 1st July.

Cox, E. (1996) *Leading Women: Tactics for Making the Difference*. Sydney: Random House.

Cross, S. & Bagilhole, B. (2002a) 'Girl's Jobs for the Boys? Men, Masculinity and Non-traditional Occupations', *Gender, Work and Organization*, 9 (2): 204–226.

Cross, S. & Bagilhole, B. (2002b) *Women in Non traditional Occupations: Challenging Men*. New York: Palgrave Macmillan.

Dalton, M. (1959) *Men who Manage*. New York: John Wiley and Son.

Davidson, M. J. & Cooper, C. L. (1983) *Stress and the Woman Manager* London: Martin Robertson.

Davidson, M. J. & Cooper, C. L. (1984) 'Occupational Stress in Female Managers: A Comparative Study', *Journal of Management Studies*, 21 (2): 185–205.

Davidson, M. & Cooper, C. (1992) *Shattering the Glass Ceiling*. London: Paul Chapman.

Dobson, I. (1997) 'No Quick Fix for Gender Imbalance', *The Australian*, 23 July: 36.

Due Billing, Y. & Alvesson, M. (1989) 'Four Ways of Looking at Women and Leadership', *Scandinavian Journal of Management*, 5 (1): 65–80.

Due Billing, Y. & Alvesson, M. (2000) 'Questioning the Notion of Feminine Leadership: A Critical Perspective on the Gender Labelling of Leadership', *Gender, Work and Organization*, 7 (3): 144–157.

du Gay, P. (1996) 'Organizing Identity: Entrepreneurial Governance and Public Management', in S. Hall and P. du Gay (Eds) *Questions of Cultural Identity*. London: Sage, pp. 151–169.

Eagly, E. & Johnson, B. (1990) 'Gender and Leadership Styles: A Meta-Analysis', *Psychological Bulletin*, 108: 233–256.

Eagly, A., Makhijani, M. & Knonsky, B. (1992) 'Gender and the Evaluation of Leaders: A Meta-Analysis', *Psychological Bulletin*, 111 (1): 3–22.

Edmonson, A. (2003) 'Speaking up in the Operating Room: How Team Leaders Promote Learning in Interdisciplinary Action Teams', *Journal of Management Studies*, 40 (6): 1419–1452.

Ely, R. (1994) 'The Social Construction of Relationships Among Professional Women at Work', in M. Davidson and R. Burke (Eds) *Women in Management: Current Research Issues*. London: Paul Chapman.

Fagenson, E. A. (1993) 'Diversity in Management: Introduction and the Importance of Women in Management', in E. A. Fagenson (Ed.) *Women in Management: Trends, Issues and Challenges in Management Diversity*. London: Sage.

Fairclough, N. (1989) *Language and Power*. Harlow: Longman.

Faludi, S. (1991) *Backlash: The Undeclared War Against American Women*. New York: Crown Publishers.

Fenwick, T. (2002) 'Transgressive Desires: New Enterprising Selves in the New Capitalism', *Work Employment and Society*, 4: 703–723.

Ferguson, K. (1984) *The Feminist Case against Bureaucracy*. Philadelphia: Temple University Press.

Ferguson, K. (1994) 'On Bringing More Theory, More Voices and More Politics to the Study of Organizations', *Organization*, 1 (1): 81–99.

Ferrario, M. (1991) 'Sex Differences in Leadership Style – Myth or Reality', *Women in Management Review*, 6 (3): 16–21.

Ferrario, M. (1994) 'Women as Managerial Leaders in Management', in M. Davidson and R. Burke (Eds) *Women in Management: Current Research Issues*. London: Paul Chapman Publishing, pp. 93–109.

Ferrario, M. & Davidson, M. J. (1991) 'Gender and Management Styles: A Comparative Study', Paper presented at British Academy of Management Conference, University of Bath.

Firestone, S. (1970) *The Dialectics of Sex*. New York: Bantam Books.

Fletcher, J. (1994) 'Castrating the Female Advantage: Feminist Standpoint Research and Management Science', *Journal of Management Inquiry*, 3 (1), March: 74–82.

Floge, L. & Merrill, D. (1986) 'Tokenism Reconsidered: Male Nurses and Female Physicians in a Hospital Setting', *Social Forces*, 64 (4): 925–947.

Fondas, N. (1996) 'Feminization at Work: Career Implications', in M. Arthur and D. Rousseau (Eds) *The Boundaryless Career*. New York: Oxford University Press.

Fondas, N. (1997) 'Feminization Unveiled: Management Qualities in Contemporary Writings', *Academy of Management Review*, 22 (1): 257–282.

Foucault, M. (1976) *Histoire de la sexualite: La volonte de savoir*. Paris: Editions Gallimard.

Gabriel, Y., Fineman, S. & Sims, D. (2000) *Organizing and Organizations*. London: Sage.

Gherardi, S. (1995) *Gender, Symbolism and Organizational Culture*. London: Sage.

Gilbert, J. A. & Ivancevich, J. M. (1999) 'Organizational Diplomacy: The Bridge for Managing Diversity', *Human Resource Planning*, 22 (3): 29–39.

Gilligan, C. (1982) *In a Different Voice: Psychological Theory and Women's Development*. Cambridge, MA: Harvard University Press.

Giroux, H. A. (1997) 'White Squall: Resistance and the Pedagogy of Whiteness', *Cultural Studies*, 11 (3): 376–389.

Goffee, R. & Scase, R. (1983) 'Business Ownership and Women's Subordination: A Preliminary Study of Female Proprietors', *The Sociological Review*, 31 (1): 625–648.

Goffee, R. & Scase, R. (1985) *Women in Charge: The Experiences of Female Entrepreneurs*. London: Allen and Unwin.

Goode, W. J. (1982) 'Why Men Resist', in B. Thorne and M. Yalom (Eds) *Rethinking the Family: Some Feminist Questions*. New York: Longman.

Gordon, N. (2002) 'On Visibility and Power: An Arendtian Corrective of Foucault', *Human Studies*, 25: 125–145.

Grant, D., Hardy, C., Oswick, C. & Putnam, L. (2004) 'Introduction: Organizational Discourse: Exploring the Field', in D. Grant, C. Hardy, C. Oswick and L. Putnam (Eds) *Organizational Discourse*, London: Sage.

Grey, C., Knights, D. & Willmott, H. (1996) 'Is a Critical Pedagogy of Management Possible', in R. French and C. Grey (Eds), *Rethinking Management Education*. London: Sage, pp. 94–110.

Hakim, C. (2000) *Work-Lifestyle Choices in the 21st Century*. New York: Oxford University Press.

Hakim, C. (2002) 'Lifestyle Preferences as Determinants of Women's Differentiated Labor Market Careers', *Work and Occupations*, 29 (4): 428–459.

Halford, S. & Leonard, P. (2001) *Gender Power and Organization: An Introduction*. Basingstoke: Palgrave.

Halford, S., Savage, M. & Witz, A. (1997) *Gender Careers and Organization: Current Developments in Banking, Nursing and Local Government*. Basingstoke: MacMillam.

Harlow, E., Hearn, J. & Parkin, W. (1995) 'Gendered Noise: Organizations and the Silence and Din of Domination', in C. Itzin and J. Newman (Eds) *Gender, Culture and Organizational Change*. London: Routledge.

Hatcher, C. (2003) 'Refashioning a Passionate Manager: Gender at Work', *Gender, Work and Organization*, 10 (4): 391–412.

Hearn, J. (1985) 'Men's Sexuality at Work' in A. Metcalf and M. Humphries (Eds) *The Sexuality of Men*. London: Pluto, pp. 110–128.

Hearn, J. (1987) The *Gender of Oppression: Men, Masculinity and the Critique of Marxism*. Brighton: Wheatsheaf.

Hearn, J. (1994) 'Changing Men and Changing Management: Social Change, Social Research and Social Action', in M. Davidson and R. Burke (Eds) *Women in Management: Current Research Issues*. London: Paul Chapman.

Hearn, J. (1996) 'Deconstructing the Dominant: Making the One(s) the Other(s)', *Organization*, 3 (4): 611–626.

Heikes, J. (1992) 'When Men are in the Minority: The Case of Men in Nursing', *The Sociological Quarterly*, 32 (3): 389–401.

Heilman, M. E. (1994): 'Affirmative Action: Some Unintended Consequences for Working Women', *Research in Organizational Behaviour*, 16: 125–169.

Hines, R. (1992) 'Accounting: Filling the Negative Space', *Accounting, Organization and Society*, 17: 314–341.

Hirschman, A. (1970) *Exit, Voice and Loyalty: Responses to Decline in Firms, Organizations and the State*. Cambridge, MA: Harvard University Press.

Hollway, C. (1994) 'Separation, Integration and Difference: Contradictions in a Gender Regime', in H. L. Radtke and H. J. Stam (Eds) *Power/Gender: Social Relations in Theory and Practice*. London: Sage.

Ibarra, H. (1993) 'Personal Networks of Women and Minorities in Management: A Conceptual Framework', *Academy of Management Review*, 18 (1): 56–87.

Jansen, G. & Davis, D. (1998) 'Honouring Voice and Visibility: Sensitive Topic Research and Feminist Interpretive Enquiry', *Affilia Journal of Women and Social Work*, 13 (3): 289–301.

Kanter, R. (1977) *Men and Women of the Corporation*. New York: Basic Books.

Kanter, R. (1989) 'The New Managerial Work', *Harvard Business Review*, 67 (6): 85–92.

Kaufman, M. (1987) 'The Construction of Masculinity and the Triad of Men's Violence' in M. Kaufman (Ed.) *Beyond Patriarchy: Essays by Men on Pleasure, Power and Change.*' Toronto: Oxford University Press.

Kaufman, M. (1994) 'Men, Feminism and Men's Contradictory Experiences of Power', in H. Brod and M. Kaufman (Eds) *Theorizing Masculinities*. London: Sage.

Kerfoot, D. & Knights, D. (1993) 'Management Masculinity and Manipulation: From Paternalism to Corporate Strategy in Financial Services in Britain', *Journal of Management Studies*, 30 (4): 659–677.

Kerfoot, D. & Knights, D. (1998) 'Managing Masculinity in Contemporary Organizational Life: A Managerial Project', *Organization*, 5 (1): 7–26.

Kerfoot, D. & Whitehead, S. (1998). 'Boy's Own Stuff: Masculinity and the Management of Further Education', *The Sociological Review*, 46: 436–537.

Kimmel, M. (1994) 'Masculinity as Homophobia: Fear, Shame and Silence in the Construction of Gender Identity', in H. Brod and M. Kaufman (Eds) *Theorising Masculinities*. London: Sage.

Konrad, A., Winter, S. & Gutek, B. (1992) 'Diversity in Work Group Sex Composition: Implications for Majority and Minority Members', *Research in Sociology of Organization*, 10: 115–140.

Kusz, K. W. (2001) 'I Want to be the Minority: The Politics of Youthful White Masculinities in Sport and Popular Culture in 1990s America', *Journal of Sport and Social Issues*, 25 (4): 390–416.

Leck, J. D. (2002) 'Making Employment Equity Programs Work for Women', *Canadian Public Policy*, XXVIII (Supplement 1): S85–S100.

Lee, C. (1994) 'The Feminization of Management', *Training*, November: 25–31.

Lee-Gosselin, M. & Grise, J. (1990) *New Reflections on the Revolution of Our Time*. London: Verso.

Leonard, P. (2002) 'Organizing Gender? Looking at Metaphors as Frames of Meaning in Gender/Organization Texts', *Gender, Work and Organization*, 9 (1): 60–80.

Lewis, A. E. (2004a): 'What Group? Studying Whites and Whiteness in the Era of Color-Blindness', *Sociological Theory*, 22 (4): 623–646.

Lewis, P. (2004b) 'Using Conflict to Highlight the Gendered Nature of Entrepreneurship: The Case of the Career Woman Entrepreneur', Paper presented at the *British Academy of Management conference*, St Andrews, September.

Lewis, P. (2006) 'The Quest for Invisibility: Female Entrepreneurs and the Masculine Norm of Entrepreneurship', *Gender, Work and Organization*, 13 (5): 453–469.

Lupton, B. (2000) 'Maintaining Masculinity: Men Who Do Women's Work', *British Journal of Management*, 11: S33–S48.

Mac An Ghaill, M. (1994) *The Making of Men*. Buckinghamshire: Open University Press.

Maddock, S. (1999) *Challenging Women: Gender Culture and Organization*. London: Sage.

Marlow, S. (1997) 'Self-Employed Women – New Opportunities, Old Challenges?', *Entrepreneurship and Regional Development*, 9: 199–210.

Marlow, J. (2000) *Votes for Women*. London: Virago Press.

Marshall, J. (1984) *Women Managers: Travellers in a Male World*. Chichester: Wiley.

Marshall, J. (1994) 'Why Women Leave Senior Management Jobs: My Research Approach and Some Initial Findings', in M. Tantum (Ed.) *Women in Management: The Second Wave*. London: Routledge.

Martin, J. (1990) 'Deconstructing Organizational Taboos: The Suppression of Gender Conflict in Organizations', *Organizational Science*, 1 (4): 339–359.

Martin, P. (2003) 'Said and Done versus Saying and Doing: Gendering Practices, Practicing Gender', *Gender and Society*, 17 (3): 342–366.

McRae, S. (2003) 'Constraints and Choices in Mothers' Employment Careers: a Consideration of Hakim's Preference Theory, *British Journal of Sociology*, 54 (3): 317–338.

Metcalfe, B. & Linstead, A. (2003) 'Gendering Teamwork: Re-writing the Feminine', *Gender, Work and Organization*, 10: 95–119.

Milliken, F., Morrison, E. & Hewlin, P. (2003) 'An Exploratory Study of Employee Silence: Issues that Employees don't Communicate Upward', *Journal of Management Studies*, 40 (6): 1453–1476.

Mills, A. (2002) 'Studying the Gendering of Organizational Culture Over Time: Issues, Concerns and Strategies', *Gender, Work and Organization*, 9 (3): 280–307.

Mills, M. (2003) 'Shaping the Boys' Agenda: The Backlash Blockbusters', *International Journal of Inclusive Education*, 7 (2): 57–73.

Mobley, M. (1992): 'Backlash! The Challenge to Diversity Training', *Training and Development*, December: 45–52.

Morgan, D. (1992) *Discovering Men*. London: Routledge.

Morgan, D. (1996) 'The Gender of Bureaucracy', in D. Collinson and J. Hearn (Eds) *Men as Managers and Managers as Men* London: Sage, pp. 46–60.

Mumby, D. & Clair, R. (1997) 'Organizational Discourse', in T. A. Van Dijk (Ed.) *Discourse as Structure and Process: Discourse Studies vol 2 – A Multidisciplinary introduction*. London: Sage, pp. 181–205.

Nicholson, N. & West, M. (1988) *Managerial Job Change: Women and Men in Transition.* Cambridge: Cambridge University Press.

Oakley, J.G. (2000) 'Gender-Based Barriers to Senior Management Positions: Understanding the Scarcity of Female CEOs', *Journal of Business Ethics*, 27: 321–334.

Olsson, S. (2000) 'Acknowledging the Female Archetype: Women Managers' Narratives of Gender', *Women in Management Review*, 15 (5/6): 296–302.

Oswick, C., Keenoy, T. & Grant, D. (2000) 'Discourse, Organizations and Organizing: Concepts, Objects and Subjects', *Human Relations*, 52 (9): 1115–1124.

Parsons, T. (1951) *The Social System*. London: Macmillan.

Piderit, S. K. & Ashford, S. J. (2003) 'Breaking Silence: Tactical Choices Women Managers Make in Speaking up About Gender-Equity Issues', *Journal of Management Studies*, 40 (6): 1477–1502.

Pierce, J. L. (2003) 'Racing for Innocence: Whiteness, Corporate Culture and the Backlash Against Affirmative Action', *Qualitative Sociology*, 26 (1): 53–70.

Potter, J. & Wetherell, M. (1987) *Discourse and Social Psychology*. London: Sage.

Powell, G. (2000) 'The Glass Ceiling: Explaining the Good and Bad News', in M. Davidson and R. Burke (Eds) *Women in Management: Current Research Issues*, Vol 2, London: Sage.

Powney, J. (1997) 'On Becoming a Manager in Education', in H. Eggins (Ed.) *Women as Leaders and Managers in Higher Education*, Milton Keynes: Open University Press.

Puwar, N. (2004) 'Thinking about Making a Difference', *British Journal of Politics and International Relations*, 6 (1): 65–80.

Rhodes, D. L. (1988) 'Perspectives on Professional Women', *Stanford Law Review*, 40 (5): 1164–1207.

Robinson, S. (2000) *Marked Men: White Masculinity in Crisis*. New York: Columbia University Press.

Rosener, J. (1990) 'Ways Women Lead', *Harvard Business Review*, Nov–Dec: 119–125.

Ross-Smith, A. & Kornberger, M. (2004) 'Gendered Rationality: A Genealogical Exploration of the Philosophical and Sociological Conceptions of Rationality, Masculinity and Organization', *Gender, Work and Organization*, 11: 280–305.

Ross-Smith, A., Kornberger, M., Anandakumar, A. & Chesterman, C. (2007) 'Women Executives: Managing Emotions at the Top', in P. Lewis and R. Simpson (Eds) *Gendering Emotions in Organizations*. Houndmills, Basingstoke: Palgrave Macmillan.

Rubin, J. (1997) 'Gender Equality and the Culture of Organizational Assessment', *Gender, Work and Organization*, 4 (1): 24–34.

Savage, M. & Witz, A. (1992) (Eds) *Gender and Bureaucracy*. Oxford: Blackwell.

Sedgwick, E. (1985) *Between Men: English Literature and Male Homosocial Desire*. New York: Columbia University Press.

Segal, L. (1990) *Slow Motion: Changing Masculinities, Changing Men*. London: Virago.

Sewell, W. H. (1992) 'A Theory of Structure: Duality, Agency and Transformation', *American Journal of Sociology*, 98 (1): 1–29.

Simpson, R. (1997) 'Have Times Changed? Career Barriers and the Token Woman Manager', *British Journal of Management*, 8: 121–129.

Simpson, R. (2000) 'Gender Mix and Organizational Fit: How Gender Imbalance at Different levels of the Organization Impacts on Women Managers', *Women In Management Review*, 15 (1): 5–20.

Simpson, R. (2004) 'Masculinities at Work: The Experiences of Men in Non-Traditional Occupations', *Work, Employment and Society*, 18 (2): 349–368.

Simpson, R. (2005) 'Seekers, Finders and Settlers: Men Who Aspire to Women's Roles', *Gender, Work and Organization*, 12 (4): 363–380 (3).

Simpson, R. and Lewis, P. (2005) 'An Investigation of Silence and a Scrutiny of Transparency: Re-Examining Gender and Organization Literature Through the Concepts of Voice and Visibility', *Human Relations*, 58 (10): 1253–1275.

Simpson, R., Sturges, J., Woods, A. & Altman, Y. (2005). 'Gender Age and the MBA: An Analysis of Extrinsic and Intrinsic Career Benefits', *Journal of Management Education*, 29: 218–247.

Singh, V. & Vinnicombe, S. (2005) *The 2005 Female FTSE Report*, Cranfield School of Management.

Smithson, J. & Stokoe, E. H. (2005) 'Discourses of Work-Life Balance: Negotiating "Genderblind" Terms in Organizations', *Gender, Work and Organization*, 12 (2): 147–168.

Tannen, D. (2001) *You Just Don't Understand: Women and Men in Conversation*. New York: Harper Collins.

The Times (2005) '*Force rejects white males*', 29 November.

Tolson, S. A. (1977) *The Limits of Masculinity*. London: Tavistock.

Tong, R. (1998) *Feminist Thought: A More Comprehensive Introduction*, 2nd edition. Boulder, CO: Westview Press.

Turnley, W. & Feldman, D. (1999) 'The Impact of Psychological Contract Violations on Exit, Voice, Loyalty and Neglect', *Human Relations*, 52 (7): 895–922.

Vinkenburg, C. J., Jansen, P. G. W. & Koopman, P. L. (2000) 'Feminine Leadership: A Review of Gender Differences in Managerial Behaviour and Effectiveness', in M. J. Davidson and R. J. Burke (Eds) *Women in Management: Current Research Issues*, Vol II. Thousand Oaks, CA: Sage, pp. 120–137.

Walby, S. (1990) *Theorising Patriarchy*. Oxford: Basil Blackwell.

Walby, S. (1997) *Gender Transformations*. London: Routledge.

Ward, J. & Winstanley, D. (2003) 'The Absent Presence: Negative Space within Discourse and the Construction of Minority Sexual Identity in the Workplace', *Human Relations*, 56 (10): 1255–1288.

West, C. & Fenstermaker, S. (1995) Doing Difference, *Gender and Society*, 9 (1): 8–37.

West, C. & Zimmerman, D. (2002) *Doing Gender, Doing Difference* London: Routledge.

Whitehead, S. (2001a) 'Woman as Manager: A Seductive Ontology', *Gender, Work and Organization*, 8 (1): 84–107.

Whitehead, S. (2001b) 'The Invisible Gendered Subject: Men in Education Management'. *Journal of Gender Studies*, 10 (1): 67–82.

Whitehead, S. & Barrett, F. (2004) 'The Sociology of Masculinity', in S. Whitehead and F. Barrett (Eds) *The Masculinities Reader*. Cambridge: Polity Press.

Whyte, W. H. (1956) *The Organization Man*. New York: Simon and Schuster.

Williams, C. (1993) (Ed.) *Doing Women's Work: Men in Non-Traditional Occupations*. London: Sage.

Wilson, F. & Thompson, P. (2001) 'Sexual Harassment as an Exercise of Power', *Gender, Work and Organization*, 8 (1): 61–83.

Woodward, K. (1997) 'Concepts of Identity and Difference', in K. Woodward (Ed.) *Identity and Difference*. London: Sage.

Wray-Bliss, E. (2002) 'Abstract Ethics, Embodied Ethics: The Strange Marriage of Foucault and Positivism in LPT', *Organization*, 9 (1): 5–39.

Yoder, J. (1991) 'Rethinking Tokenism: Looking Beyond Numbers', *Gender and Society*, 5 (1): 178–192.

Yoder, J. (1994) 'Looking Beyond Numbers: The Effects of Gender Status, Job Prestige and Occupational Gender –Typing on Tokenism Processes', *Social Psychology Quarterly*, 57 (2): 150–159.

Young, I. M. (1994) 'Gender as Seriality: Thinking about Woman as a Social Collective', *Signs: Journal of Women in Culture and Society*, 19 (3): 713–738.

Zimmer, L. E. (1988) 'Tokenism and Women in the Workplace: the Limits of Gender Neutral Theory', *Social Problems*, 35: 64–77.

Author index

West, C., 16–17, 26
West, M., 2
Whitehead, S., 28, 51, 60, 65, 72, 73, 75
Whyte, W. H., 11, 50
Williams, C., 41, 45, 46, 48, 49
Wilson, F., 35
Winstanley, D., 34, 35
Witz, A., 89

Woodward, K., 53
Wray-Bliss, E., 84

Yoder, J., 45
Young, I. M., 62

Zimmer, L. E., 41, 45
Zimmerman, D., 16–17, 26

Subject index

gendered nature, 27, 45, 60, 64
group size/composition, 38
Other, the, 61, 62, 72
othering, 34, 53, 84

patriarchy, 5, 6, 31, 32, 66, 78
pay, 53, 54, 58, 69
performance pressure, 83
performances of gender, 27
performative model, 16
performativity, 27
phallocentric model, 11
pipeline theory, 43
polarization, 40–1, 47
post-structuralism, 6–8, 23, 73–9, 81,
    89, 90
    and discourse, 25, 36
power, 12, 31, 33, 58, 89
    relations, 32, 52, 64, 68, 69
preference theory, 20
psychic hardening, 69
psychoanalytical approaches, 71–3, 79

Queen Bee syndrome, 42, 43, 44

radical feminism, 5–6, 8, 15, 23, 89, 90
rationality, 29
re-masculinization, 14
research, 2, 5, 15, 17, 22, 83
rhetoric, 31, 33, 34, 84
role(s)
    female, 41, 42, 43
    leadership, 67
    male, 47, 48, 65
    sex, 33, 67
    stereotypical, 14, 42
    theory, 67, 68, 73
    traps, 41, 44, 83

sameness, 19–21
seriality, 62, 63
sex integration, 43–4
sexism, 33
sexual harassment, 41
sexual identities, 34
silence, 18, 34, 36, 77, 84
    and discourse, 33–6, 86

silence
    and din, 18, 19, 23
    and invisibility, 3, 4
silencing, process of, 36, 49
socialization, 68
socializing agents, 67
social relations perspective, 68–71, 73, 78–9
'space invaders', 60
stereotypical roles, 14, 20, 42, 47
stereotyping, 44, 83
Suffragette movement, 33
surface/deep conceptualizations, voice and
    visibility, 82
surface conceptualizations, 4, 8, 10, 17, 21
    voice and visibility, 4–5, 26, 49, 67, 78

team-working, 31
tipping, 53
token status, 2, 6, 39, 41, 49
    and high visibility, 40, 42–3, 69, 87
    male, 46, 47, 48
transactional leadership, 67
transformational leadership, 12–13, 16, 22, 24, 89

victimization, 59
victims, 58–60, 88
visibility, 2, 3, 37, 38, 48, 49
    and group dynamics, 39
    high, 40
    men, 46
    reduced, 44
    and role traps, 42
victim, 58, 88
    see also voice and visibility
voice
    women, 15, 19, 32
    and visibility, 2–8, 9, 22, 81, 82, 89–90

'week-end warriors', 77
women
    in senior positions, 13, 19, 44
    as victims, 54
women's voice(s), 10, 15–17
    perspective, 22
    research, 5, 17
women's voice literature, 2, 6, 11, 17, 22, 82
    solution/resolution, 19, 21, 22